ST. ANDREWS & GOLF

ST. ANDREWS & GOLF

◆ With Illustrations by ARTHUR WEAVER◆

Morton W. Olman and John M. Olman

Market Street Press
Cincinnati ◆ Edinburgh

ALSO FROM MARKET STREET PRESS:

The Encyclopedia of Golf Collectibles

Golf Antiques & Other Treasures of the Game (revised edition)

Olmans' Guide to Golf Antiques

The Squire: The Legendary Golfing Life of Gene Sarazen

◆

Library of Congress Cataloging-in-Publication Data

Olman, Morton W.
    St. Andrews & Golf / Morton W. Olman and John M. Olman; with
illustrations by Arthur Weaver. — 1st ed.
    p. cm.
    Includes bibliographical references and index
    LCCN: 93-78338
    ISBN: 0-942117-20-4
    1. Royal and Ancient Golf Club of St. Andrews — Pictorial works.
2. Golf — Scotland — St. Andrews — Pictorial works. 3. St. Andrews (Fife) —
Pictorial works. 4. British Open Golf Championship. 5. Golf — History.
I. Olman, John M. II. Weaver, Arthur, ill. III. Title. IV. Title: St. Andrews and
Golf. V. Title: Saint Andrews and Golf.

GV969.R6056 1995   796.352'09413'3

◆

For bulk book sales and lithographs by Arthur Weaver, contact:

United States: United Kingdom and Europe:
Market Street Press   Old Golf Shop
325 West Fifth Street   13 Albany Street
Cincinnati, Ohio 45202   Edinburgh, Scotland EH1 3PY
1-800-433-1000   0800-891-527

Dedicated to those unknown individuals who first played golf on the links of St. Andrews some 500 years ago.

EDITORIAL CONTRIBUTIONS

Essays about St. Andrews have been graciously provided by the following Open and Amateur champions, writers and golf luminaries:

CONTENTS

*I*t's easy to envision a talented golf artist as a frustrated golfer, one who has turned to brush and palette after realizing that he can't tame the game with a club and ball. But Englishman Arthur Weaver — regarded by many as the dean of modern golf artists — is just the opposite of this stereotype. It's difficult to believe, but Weaver does not, has not and never intends to play golf. He merely enjoys the beauty of the game.

Weaver's keen perception of the game has made his golf course paintings favorites for nearly 40 years. Since his watercolor depiction of Royal Liverpool Golf Club (Hoylake) was reproduced as an art print in 1957, approximately

three dozen of his works have been offered as short-run, limited edition lithographs. Many scenes depict major championships at famous venues, including the Old Course at St. Andrews, Muirfield, Augusta National and Pebble Beach. While the golfers in the scenes are often minuscule in size, Weaver's attention to detail captures the characteristic poses of such stars as Lee Trevino, Jack Nicklaus and Nick Faldo.

What many connoisseurs of golf art don't realize is that Weaver is experienced in all phases of painting. Since graduating from the Hornsey School of Art (near London) in 1938, he has worked in various fields — from painting theater sets and industrial subjects such as railroads, diamond mines, castles, and oil wells to doing newspaper illustrations and painting portraits. He's done other sporting subjects besides golf, such as hunting, fishing, curling and ice hockey.

But golf art is Weaver's claim to fame and since the early 1970s, his paintings and lithographs have been featured in galleries on both sides of the Atlantic. Original works can be viewed at the U.S. Golf Association Museum in Far Hills, New Jersey, and at prominent golf clubs throughout the world.

This book contains 225 illustrations, including a few of Weaver's early scenes from the 1950s and '60s.

Weaver was born in North London in 1918, and currently resides in Wales with his wife, Margaret.

8

INTRODUCTION

The idea for this book came from a drawing no larger than a golf ball. Eleven years ago, as we viewed some lithographs of golf scenes painted by Arthur Weaver, we became intrigued by the remarques in the bottom margins. (A remarque is a small drawing done by the artist that adds a distinctive embellishment to an art print.) Weaver's remarques were simple, with a minimum of pencil strokes, but were amazingly accurate in conveying the rhythm of a golf swing or the slope of a putting green.

Weaver had done several paintings for clients of our golf art and antiques business, the Old Golf Shop. During a meeting, we mentioned our fascination with his remarques. We asked for permission to reproduce some for the chapter headings of *The Encyclopedia of Golf Collectibles*, a book we were writing at the time. Weaver was so enthusiastic about the idea that he sketched three special views of the Old Course, Augusta National and Cypress Point.

In the late 1980s, Weaver painted a series of portraits of early Open champions, which we reproduced as prints. Some of the editions were limited to 350 prints, and Weaver remarqued each with a different thumbnail drawing. On the Old Tom Morris prints, for instance, many of the remarques were related to Morris, such as golf balls and clubheads marked with his imprint, and the Open Championship belt and trophy. The sketches were small and quick, but contained incredible detail.

As the prints sold, customers related how much they enjoyed the remarques. We mentioned this to Weaver in 1989 and brainstormed about how to produce an illustrated book.

It didn't take long to pick St. Andrews as the subject; it was a natural. There is something about St. Andrews that captivates golfers and nongolfers alike. At first, it seems like just another old town. But the more you walk around, meet people and discover its history, the more you fall in love with it. We hope that through our research, writing and editing, and through Weaver's pencil, pen and brush that you, too, will discover what makes St. Andrews such a special place.

John (left) and Mort Olman in the garden of Old Tom Morris' home.

Morton W. Olman
John M. Olman
May 1995

The Town

Fishermen's houses along North Street, early 1500s.

*In medieval times, St. Andrews was recognized
as a center of religion and higher learning.*

AN ENGLISHMAN'S VIEW

by Peter Dobereiner

Englishman Peter Dobereiner, a longtime British newspaper golf correspondent, currently writes a monthly column and other articles for Golf Digest *(USA) and* Golf World *(UK). A resident of Kent, he has authored 20 books on golf.*

On my first visit to St. Andrews, friends had persuaded me that an essential part of the golf experience was to engage the services of a caddie. My man was a dour and reticent old fellow who seemed to regard a round of the Old Course as some kind of religious ritual. By the time we reached the 17th, his soul had been soured by my pagan inability to identify the church spire at which he bade me aim my drive.

At last, on the 17th tee, we had a secular landmark for the target line. "Hit your drive directly over the letter *D*," he commanded, indicating the name *Anderson* painted on the roof of the old railway sheds. I went one better and my ball hit the letter *D* fairly and squarely, rebounding into oblivion. I remember, with a pang of shame, that I subsequently described the Old Course as a "sad old bitch of a golf course" in the public prints.

By contrast, I fell in love with the city at first sight from the window of the fussy, little train which conveyed me from Leuchars after the overnight sleeper from London. This is how medieval cities should look, I thought, compact and free of suburban clutter. When the university built residence halls to spoil that approaching view of St. Andrews, I was distressed that an academic institution could inflict such barbarism upon the landscape. My feelings when those railway sheds were replaced by the Old Course Hotel are best not described.

With the exception of these unfortunate aberrations, and a few others, St. Andrews seems to me to do a pretty good job of preserving its historical and architectural integrity while accommodating itself to contemporary life. Most of us have the opportunity only to walk the streets and enjoy the facades of the ancient buildings. But that word *facade* is a misnomer for, in many cases, the buildings stand with their backs against the public streets. Penetrate those facades and you discover the true beauty of the architecture, set off by splendid, walled gardens and trim lawns. In this sense of mystery and unsuspected delights, the city is at one with the Old Course. It takes time and patience to get to know them and only when you know them thoroughly can you truly appreciate them.

But without people, a golf course is just another piece of landscape, pleasing enough to the eye in some cases but no more so than its surroundings. It is much the same with buildings. Populate St. Andrews with Hottentots or Patagonians and it would not be the same place. You may say that people are people and we are all the same under the skin. It is a noble thought which does you credit, but except on a most superficial level it is arrant nonsense. The Scots are a separate people like no other, a race apart with their own distinctive values, and virtues and vices. And the people of East Fife are different from those of Edinburgh, Glasgow, Aberdeen, the western isles or the borders. Subdivided even further and the people of St. Andrews are different from those who live a few miles away in the fishing ports of Pittenweem, Anstruther and Leven.

Within my own genetic cocktail the major ingredient, albeit a paltry 25 percent, is blood from the Robertsons of Hellensburgh (west of Glasgow). In my naive, romantic way, I fancied I might be accepted, at least as a prodigal second cousin. I was soon disabused of such wishful thinking and forced to endure the second class status of a "furriner." It may be a universal trait to delight in taking foreigners for a ride, but there is a type of Scot who seems to regard the clipping of foreigners, far from being dishonest, as no less than a patriotic duty.

In St. Andrews, of course, golf opens all doors. For a really great player like Bobby Jones, golf can also open all hearts. In my case a small reputation as a chronicler of the game provided entre into the brotherhood of golf. Not as wide a circle as you might imagine, for the Scots have an acute perception of the difference between a real golf person and someone who plays at golf.

For a full appreciation of St. Andrews and all that it represents, the visitor must have a sense of history. Few people have been privileged as I was to go through a time warp, back to the age of the Stuart kings, as I stood alongside Laurie Auchterlonie in his clubmaking workshop for a week. He initiated me into the ancient crafts of shaping and gouging hornbeam heads, cutting and pegging ram's horn inserts and gluing the splice. Now, aided by this book, we can all go through a time warp and savour every aspect of St. Andrews through the ages.

THE EARLY DAYS

According to archaeological studies in and around St. Andrews, strategic location of the town on the Eden River and St. Andrews Bay and surrounding fertile farmland attracted the Romans, Picts, Culdees and other ancient civilizations. Organized government came in 1141, when the town was recognized as a burgh by King David I. The cathedral was founded in 1160, and the university — the oldest in Scotland — traces its beginnings to the early 1400s. The castle for the bishop was built in 1200.

Much of St. Andrews still resembles a medieval town. It was laid out on three somewhat parallel east-west thoroughfares: North, Market and South streets. Although some examples of architecture from the 15th and 16th centuries remain, most of the old sandstone buildings were erected in the 18th and 19th centuries.

Scottish history books are filled with details of religious conflicts. After Christianity came to the area around 565, St. Andrews grew into the ecclesiastical center of Scotland. There are accounts of how the Catholics battled the Episcopalians and how the Protestants later fought for their beliefs during the Reformation. Today, monuments in town recall the deeds of famous martyrs.

The Eden Estuary, the broad, shallow mouth of the Eden River where it meets the North Sea, just north of the links.

The cultivation and harvesting of mussels in the Eden Estuary went on for centuries until the 1940s, when profitability suffered due to increasing labor and shipping costs.

For nearly a thousand years — until the beginning of this century — fishing was the main industry in St. Andrews. The fleet endured fierce seas and deadly storms, but finally succumbed to a weak economy.

15

Once there were many more fishermen than golfers in St. Andrews. Now the opposite is true.

A few commercial boats are the only remaining link to the once flourishing seafood industry, which diminished in the early 20th century. Here, the lobster catch is unloaded at the harbor.

The "fisherfolk" had their own community situated between the castle and the cathedral. The area, presently known as Ladyhead, featured small stone houses. While the men were at sea, the fisherwomen, in their colorful garb and long aprons, worked outdoors mending nets and sails (the first motorized fishing boat wasn't used until 1911).

The harbor, as seen from the Abbey wall, now provides a safe haven for recreational sailboats. Built circa 1100 at the mouth of the Kinness Burn to protect boats from the strong currents of St. Andrews Bay, the harbor has been reconstructed several times. A recycling effort took place in the mid-1600s, when the Long Pier was repaired using timbers and stones salvaged from the crumbling walls of the castle and cathedral.

Although St. Andrews is known to most as a golfer's mecca, it's really a college town: the University of St. Andrews dominates the architectural landscape. With university buildings and students everywhere, it's hard to believe that enrollment is only about 5,000. Perhaps this intimacy is what has attracted students and educators for nearly 600 years.

The chapel of St. Leonard's College remains part of the university. With part of the structure dating to the 12th century, it underwent improvements in the 1540s, 1853, 1910 and was extensively renovated between 1948 and 1952.

The University of St. Andrews is home to the oldest library in Scotland. Robert Smart, keeper of the muniments, is entrusted with the care of its extensive archives.

American statesman and inventor Benjamin Franklin received a Doctor of Laws degree from the university in 1759. He also was awarded the Freedom of the City — an exclusive, honorary citizenship.

PROMINENT UNIVERSITY

Although golfers may argue otherwise, St. Andrews is more of a college town than a holiday spot. The University of St. Andrews traces its beginnings to 1410, when Bishop Wardlaw saw a need for higher education and established Scotland's first center of higher learning. Formal charters and papal decrees followed soon thereafter.

The university's makeup is quite complex. Its notable colleges were founded long ago: St. Salvator's (1450), St. Leonard's (1512) and St. Mary's (1537). Other colleges include United College, a merger of St. Leonard's and St. Salvator's College in 1747, and St. John's College, which was started in the early 1400s and absorbed into St. Mary's in 1540. To add to the confusion, St. Leonard's is now a boarding school for girls, and Madras College, founded in 1833 on South Street, is a grade school.

Today, both historic and contemporary university buildings are interspersed throughout the city center and outlying landscape. A current enrollment of about 5,000 enjoys extensive research facilities and a personalized education, perpetuating St. Andrews' reputation as a center of education.

St. Leonard's School for Girls, an independent school for boarders and day students, was founded in 1877. The buildings at the east end of South Street, some of which are 400 years old, were once home to St. Leonard's College, part of the University of St. Andrews. The 30-acre campus incorporates several historic structures including Queen Mary's House — reputed to be the home of Mary, Queen of Scots — which was restored in 1927 for use as the school library.

St. Mary's College was founded in 1537 to promote the study of theology at the university. This is the Principal's Residence, built in 1744.

Sir Hugh Lyon Playfair, provost of St. Andrews from 1842 to 1861, was the driving force in reviving the town from a century-and-a-half of neglect.

Major Playfair purchased this building from St. Leonard's College in 1827 for use as his residence. His magnificent, private garden, replete with 90-foot-high pagoda, fountains, water-driven contrivances and sculptures, was a popular tourist attraction. In 1882, the property became part of the St. Leonard's School for Girls.

PLAYFAIR REVITALIZED ST. ANDREWS

Sir Hugh Lyon Playfair (1786-1861) did more for the well-being of St. Andrews than any other person in history. As provost (mayor) from 1842 to 1861, he instituted public works projects such as gas lighting, street paving and harbor enhancement. Playfair was a master at raising funds from the public and private sectors, and at generating income for the city. He was responsible for the construction of the town hall, a new slaughterhouse, the Martyr's Monument, expansion of several educational facilities, and for golfers: a new Union Parlour and the current clubhouse of the R & A.

His civic work followed a distinguished military career in India, where he served in the Bengal Horse Artillery and attained the rank of major. Born near Dundee, he briefly attended the university, where his father was Principal of the United College. For his contributions to improving the standard of life in St. Andrews, Playfair received an honorary doctorate from the university and was knighted by Her Majesty, both in 1856.

For 700 years, until 1862, the Tolbooth stood in the center of Market Street. At this town hall, taxes were collected, public meetings were held, and lawbreakers were celled and/or tortured. Markets were held at the adjacent Mercat Cross, and commodities were weighed at the public weigh beam known as the Tron.

24

The "new" Town Hall on South Street, as seen from the Church of the Holy Trinity, was completed in 1861. Town Council met here until local government was transferred to the North East Fife District Council in Cupar in 1974. Today the building houses the Burgh's artifacts and serves as a public meeting place.

This wood escutcheon of the town's coat of arms was salvaged from the Church of the Holy Trinity, which was rebuilt in 1799. The carving, now in the Town Hall (far left), depicts the town's namesake — the apostle Andrew — and an oak tree and boar signifying the nearby Boar's Chase region, once the hunting ground of Scottish kings.

LOCAL GOVERNMENT

Inhabitants of St. Andrews have experienced various forms of government since man came to the Fife region thousands of years ago. The Romans, who had several forts in the area by A.D. 90, were among the early rulers. When Christianity arrived in the sixth century, the land was governed by the Celtic church and its bishops. In about 1141, King David I created the Burgh of St. Andrews under the auspices of Bishop Robert. Since the 14th century, citizens have had representation in Parliament.

For eight centuries, St. Andrews town was governed by the burghal system: an elected town council headed by a provost. The best known of the provosts was Hugh Lyon Playfair, who brought the town back from near-ruin in the mid-19th century.

The Reform Act of 1918 and subsequent Parliamental legislation regionalized local government. Since 1974, the town has been governed by the joint efforts of the Fife Regional Council, the North East Fife District Council and the Community Council.

Population has ranged from as many as 14,000 residents some 500 years ago when St. Andrews was the ecclesiastical capital of Scotland under the Roman Church, to less than 2,000 in the early 18th century when religious rule was transferred to Glasgow and Edinburgh. The current population is expanding, with 15,000 residents plus about 5,000 university students.

In the northeast corner of town, on a cliff overlooking the bay, are the stone ruins of the castle. Originally constructed circa 1200, it served as a fortress and palace for the bishop and visiting royalty. Since the structure was rebuilt numerous times following attacks by dissidents, the remaining ruins date primarily to the 16th century. A popular tourist attraction is the Bottle Dungeon, a deep pit carved into the native rock.

The initials "PH" in the sidewalk near St. Salvator's Tower on North Street mark the spot where Patrick Hamilton was burned at the stake in 1528. Found guilty of heresy by the Catholic Church for his Lutheran beliefs, Hamilton was the first martyr of the Scottish Reformation.

The Market Street fountain — now a planter — was erected in memory of George Whyte-Melville (1821-1878), a Victorian novelist and poet, as well as avid golfer and hunter. It is centered in the cobblestone street, once the site of the burgh's Tolbooth, a town hall where taxes were collected and prisoners were incarcerated and executed as far back as the 12th century. Until 1768, the site also featured the Mercat Cross, a monument indicating the location of the weekly farmers' market, and the public weighing scale. Vendors continue the tradition today by setting up an open-air market.

28

The West Port Arch (above and right) was rebuilt over South Street in 1589 to mark the entrance to the city. Depicted above the opening are the coats of arms of the town and of King David I.

◆

"Most of us have the opportunity only to walk the streets and enjoy the facades of the ancient buildings. But that word 'facade' is a misnomer for, in many cases, the buildings stand with their backs against the public streets."

— *Peter Dobereiner*

◆

30

A palm tree in Scotland? Yes, even though the latitude of St. Andrews places it 1,000 miles north of Boston, the warm waters of the nearby Gulf Stream cause relatively mild winters, thus allowing this botanical oddity to endure in a garden on Queen's Terrace.

A doo-cot — or dovecote — is an elaborate nesting place for keeping pigeons prior to consumption. This one, of typical Scottish stone construction, is incorporated into a garden wall.

The 2-foot diameter Blue Stane (or Stone) was believed to have had mystical and superstitious qualities for nearly 2,000 years. After changing sites several times, it now rests near Kate's Bar at the corner of Alexandra Place and St. Mary's Place.

Adventurous tourists — those who dare to venture beyond the prominent public attractions — will find a plethora of charming features tucked away down alleys and side streets.

This 500-year-old yew tree grows in a private garden on South Street. In addition to many elaborate private gardens, the town is home to the 18-acre University Botanic Garden.

◆

Nowhere in town is there more of a spiritual link with history than at the ruins of the magnificent cathedral, which dates to the 12th century, and the 11th-century St. Rules Tower. Abandoned and desecrated after the Protestant Reformation in 1559, the grounds have since served as a cemetery and park. Here, visitors can observe the graves of the legends of St. Andrews: Morris, Robertson, Philp, Playfair, Auchterlonie…

◆

The tombstone of golf legend Young Tom Morris (1851-1875) overlooks the graves of his father, Old Tom, and other family members.

Allan Robertson's tombstone features a bust and crossed clubs. The noted ballmaker and best player of his era never won the Open Championship — he died in 1859, one year before the inaugural contest.

Hugh Philp, the Stradivarius of clubmakers, was buried in 1856.

The 108-foot-high St. Rules Tower and neighboring cathedral ruins, as seen from the castle.

34

Until recently, a bagpiper regularly marched down The Scores to the Martyrs' Monument playing a selection of traditional tunes.

A young boy parades his donkeys along Granny Clark's Wynd, a narrow public street that cuts across the 18th and first fairways of the Old Course.

Ever since Provost Playfair established sanitary standards for the town over a century ago, St. Andrews has enjoyed a tradition of tidiness.

A leisurely wait for the bus.

CHRISTIE SPREADS THE WORD

If you need information about an 18th-century St. Andrean, Gordon Christie is the one to ask. If he can't find it in his files or personal library, he'll visit the newspaper or university archives.

Gordon Christie

No one person is more concerned with the history and future of St. Andrews than Gordon Christie. This octogenarian has enjoyed a lifelong passion for researching the town's storied history and has voluntarily served as its goodwill ambassador for two decades.

If you need information about an 18th-century St. Andrean, Christie is the one to ask. If he can't find it in his files or personal library, he'll visit the newspaper or university archives. The local newspaper called him "St. Andrews' unofficial public relations man," but he's also a walking encyclopedia.

Christie travels frequently — to America, China and the Continent — but always returns to St. Andrews, his family's home for five generations. He's flown on the supersonic Concorde, but his flight as a 5-year-old in an open cockpit three-seater is more memorable. It took place on a historical occasion: during the area's first civil air display, conducted over the West Sands in 1919.

It's no surprise that he can recall this early means of transportation. Christie's life has centered around wheeled vehicles: his father and uncle were proprietors of Christie Brothers, Motor and Cycle Engineers. Opened as a bicycle and motorcycle shop in 1906, they expanded it to include automobiles a few years later.

The elder Christie also was Burgh firemaster from 1921 to 1941. And when Gordon qualified for his driver's license in 1931, he got to drive the fire tender: "a 1921 Maxwell touring car," he remembers. The endeavors of the Christie brothers provided young Gordon with plenty of excitement. They were responsible for conducting the Scottish Motorcycle Speed Championships on the West Sands for 20 years.

When not assisting with the family business, Gordon managed to get a basic education at Madras College.

The Great Depression brought a demise to Christie Brothers, but Gordon resurrected it in 1936 when he opened a bicycle shop. During World War II, it was no surprise that Christie served in the Royal Air Force as an engine fitter. His parents managed the shop in his absence. In 1955 he relocated the shop to 86 Market Street, where bicycles and toys were sold.

Christie sold the business in 1975 so he could devote more time to research and travel. Long active in the St. Andrews Merchants' Association, he was responsible for the production of a street map and town history which the merchants could distribute to tourists. He remains active in the annual St. Andrews Day celebration, the St. Andrews Preservation Trust and the St. Andrews Overseas Society.

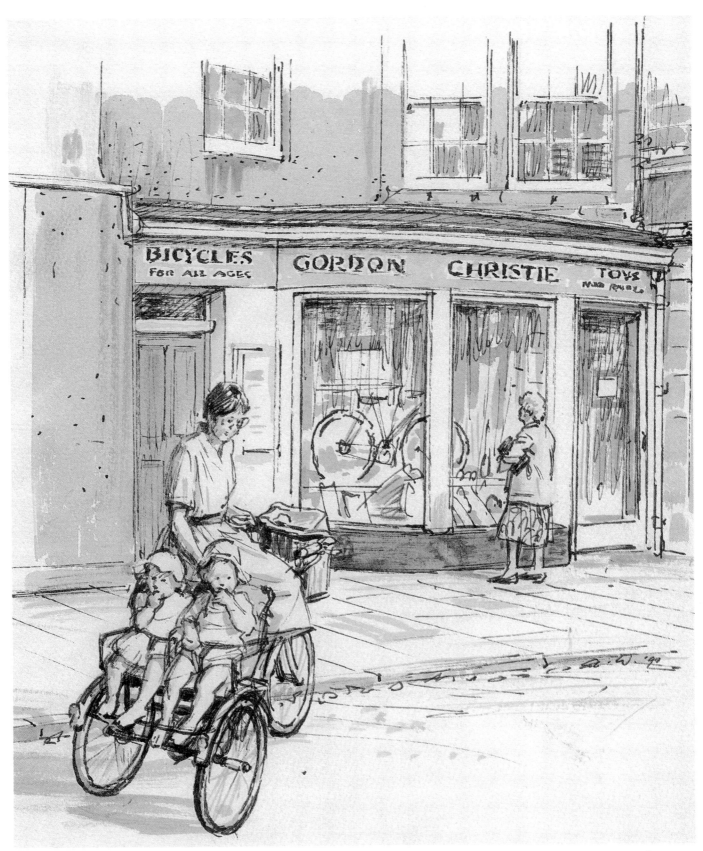

A child's paradise! From Matchbox cars to Thomas the Tank Engine and Paddington Bear, Gordon Christie's on Market Street was the place to shop for 40 years. Now on South Street, the business continues to carry the Christie name.

The Jigger Inn, originally the stationmaster's house abutting the train station and railway along the Road Hole, now nestles up to the Old Course Hotel. The pub (also pictured at far right) is popular with golfers and caddies.

The Keys, a pub frequented by many of the town's veteran caddies, is on Market Street near the fountain.

The start of footrace during a Highland games competition at the university.

A picnic among the dunes of the West Sands is a relaxing alternative to golf on a sunny afternoon.

The Niblick, on Golf Place, offers fine dining upstairs and a pub downstairs.

St. Andreans look forward to the festive Kate Kennedy Pageant each April and the centuries-old Lammas Fair in August.

The St. Andrews Woollen Mill, a wedge shot from the 18th green of the Old Course, is the most popular apparel shop in St. Andrews. Featuring knitwear at sale prices, it's difficult for visitors to leave empty-handed. (Golf historians, take note: This building was once home to R. Forgan & Son, the famous clubmakers. Outside, you can still see the firm's name embedded in the sidewalk.)

The 125-room St. Andrews Old Course Hotel is situated along the 17th hole. Complete with spa and swimming pool, it offers the most luxurious lodging in town. The hotel was built on the site of the old railway and drying sheds and opened in 1968. Immediately there grew a controversy over its garish facade. Ownership changed several times in the ensuing years as the project suffered from financial and management woes. The current ownership consortium purchased the hotel in the late 1980s and performed a massive renovation. When the Old Course Hotel reopened in 1990, it had a totally new — and non-controversial — exterior.

Inset above: *Rusack's Marine Hotel, with a commanding view of the 18th hole, was opened by William Rusack in 1887. The establishment has been patronized by scores of notables, including the Prince of Wales, Bobby Jones, Peter Thomson and Sean Connery. Rusack's is now owned by the Trusthouse Forte hotel chain.*

◆

Since Victorian times, tourists have flocked to St. Andrews for golf and sea bathing. In addition to virtually every famous golfer, notable visitors have included the crown heads of Europe, socialites such as the Vanderbilts and Rothschilds, and entertainers Bing Crosby and Sean Connery.

◆

The Royal Hotel had its own horse-drawn taxi to transport visitors to and from the train station in the late 19th century.

In the 1840s, St. Andrews was the hotbed of photographic experimentation in Scotland. The efforts of David Brewster, Hugh Lyon Playfair, John and Robert Adamson, and Tom Rodger left us with priceless images of the town and its people. While these gentlemen worked with lenses and chemistry, artist Thomas Hodge used a brush and paper scraps to record his impressions.

Thomas Hodge (1827-1907), a schoolmaster by profession, made thousands of watercolor sketches depicting 19th-century life in St. Andrews. He was a member of the R & A, where he won several gold medals in the 1860s. A keen sportsman, the well-liked Englishman also excelled at billiards, riflery and fishing. Hodge's golf illustrations, usually signed "TH" with the date, are prized by museums and collectors.

In the 1850s, Thomas Hodge opened a boarding school for boys in this house on Queen's Terrace. He eventually sold the school, choosing to devote full time to his pastime of illustrating.

47

IMAGES OF OLD ST. ANDREWS

In the 1830s, the craft of photography was in its infancy. Englishman William Henry Fox Talbot and Frenchman Louis J.M. Daguerre were both experimenting with methods for making permanent photographs, unbeknownst to each other. Daguerre succeeded first; his Daguerreotype, patented in 1839, exhibited exceptional clarity. But it had a major drawback: there was no means for duplicating the positive images that were exposed directly onto treated glass plates.

Fox Talbot, on the other hand, invented a process whereby a translucent paper negative was produced, which then could generate multiple prints. This Talbot-type or calotype process intrigued many scientifically

Thomas Rodger (1832-1883) learned photography while a medical student and lab assistant to Dr. Adamson. At the age of 16, he opened the first professional studio in St. Andrews, which remained a family business until the 1920s.

48

A medical doctor by profession, Dr. John Adamson (1810-1870) was a pioneer in the development of the calotype process of photography. He became fascinated with the novel method of producing paper photographs while teaching chemistry and science at Madras College in the late 1830s.

Press photographer George Cowie, shown with an example from his antique camera collection, recorded St. Andrews and its citizenry from the 1930s until his death in 1982. More than 100,000 of his images make up "The George Cowie Collection" at the University Library.

oriented people, including Sir David Brewster of St. Andrews. Brewster corresponded with and visited Fox Talbot to learn more about his patented method.

Brewster, in turn, shared his photographic knowledge with fellow St. Andreans Major Hugh Lyon Playfair and Dr. John Adamson. Successful picture-taking was a far cry from today's "point-and-shoot" methods. It was not uncommon for their bulky tripod-mounted cameras to require exposures of up to five minutes. Undaunted, the three began to record much of the town's sights and personalities.

Fox Talbot, meanwhile, sought to expand the market for calotypes. He wrote to Brewster in 1842 telling him of his desire to have a professional calotypist in Scotland. Brewster turned to his friend, Dr. Adamson. Adamson had taught his younger brother, Robert, the process and persuaded him to set up shop with David Hill, another pioneer photographer, in Edinburgh. Their significant partnership lasted from 1843 to 1848, when Robert died unexpectedly.

Dr. Adamson considered taking over his brother's business, but a scarcity of physicians in St. Andrews convinced him to remain in the town. This decision enabled him to develop his medical practice and pursue his interest in curbing cholera and other infectious diseases.

To keep the art of photography on a positive course, Dr. Adamson encouraged a young medical student, Thomas Rodger, to set up business as a professional calotypist in St. Andrews. The talented Rodger was

Sir David Brewster (1781-1868), credited with introducing photography to St. Andrews in the mid-19th century, is best known as the inventor of the kaleidoscope, which he patented in 1817.

only 16 years old when he opened his studio. Because prints, as well as negatives, were made in bright sunlight, a garden at the west end of town provided the ideal workplace.

The young photographer was to become very successful. In 1853 he

began winning awards, and in 1877 he won a medal at the prestigious International Photographic Competition. In 1864-65, when *The Kingdom of Fife* was published, it included lithographs taken from calotypes by Rodger. His greatest distinction, though, was working for Queen Victoria and the Duke of Edinburgh in the 1870s.

Rodger moved his studio several times and eventually settled at 6 St. Mary's Place, now part of St. Andrews University. Like most of the early calotypists, he had switched to the simpler wet-plate process in the 1860s. After Rodger's death in 1883, his son, George, carried on the business until just after the turn-of-the-century. Sadly, after the studio closed, workmen reportedly destroyed all of the glass negatives left behind. (Another son, John, was a photographer in nearby Broughty Ferry.)

The most outstanding "modern" photography in St. Andrews can be attributed to George Cowie and his wife, Beatrice Govan Cowie. George was a press photographer, covering everything from golf matches to royal visits, and received most of the notoriety of the pair. Beatrice, an accomplished portrait photographer, chose to do much of the behind-the-scenes duties in the darkroom. Together they operated Cowie & Govan, a studio and photo shop on South Street, until George's death in 1982.

Like Brewster, Adamson, Rodger and others before him, Cowie was a master with film and lens. Their images remain today as an invaluable link with old St. Andrews and her people.

Sir David Brewster's residence was in the south building of St. Leonard's College. It now is part of St. Leonard's School.

The Golf

Golfers approaching the famous Road Hole during practice rounds before the 1964 Open Championship.

The links of St. Andrews have been home to golf for more than 500 years.

A Scribe's Admiration

by Dick Taylor

Dick Taylor was editor-in-chief of Golf World *(USA) from 1962 to 1989. He now writes for six magazines in three countries and does television golf commentary.*

*I*n the winter of 1932 my parents told me we were going to the 1933 World's Fair in Chicago come summertime. Never had I anticipated such a happening in my preteen life. Not even Christmas.

In the spring of 1964, as editor of *Golf World*, I scheduled myself to cover my first Open…in St. Andrews. Only back then I called it the "British" Open. Never had I anticipated so much since 1933 and the World's Fair. Scotland! The Open! St. Andrews!

In the South, where I live, that's called "hog heaven." I was not disappointed. St. Andrews is to golf what the Vatican is to Catholics, the Louvre is to art lovers, the Alps are to skiers.

I have been to all the Open Championships since held at St. Andrews, and each time it is an even bigger thrill. It's like coming home after a long absence. In the 1980s, my wife was able to accompany me to two St. Andrews Opens, and the second time around for her was more intense than the first. As we drove through Auchtermuchty she was like all children on a trip. "Are we there yet?" she kept asking.

Rounding that final bend, when the old red-brick hotel/dorm and Royal and Ancient clubhouse loomed on the horizon, she quite literally began to shout,

"There it is! There it is!" (Mind you, her antecedents are pure English. The prime minister lives on the street named after her benevolent forbearers.)

We had spent three weeks in Fife in 1984, thinking we would use it as a base to travel around, but never left town. St. Andreans and those who love the "auld grey toun" know why.

When Jack Nicklaus failed to qualify for the final 36 holes at Muirfield in 1992, he wasn't sure he'd ever return for the Open and understandably. The degenerate disc in the neck he had lived with all his life was catching up to him, and he played that season with a numb leg. I insisted that he promise to play in 1995. "Why should I?" he asked. I answered, "It's at St. Andrews and I'll be 70, and so it probably will be my last Open."

Bless him, he said, "In that case, I'll be there." But it was the lure of St. Andrews that got him, not me. He may have affection for Muirfield, where he won his first championship, but when he won his last at St. Andrews, tears were streaming down his face as he made that magical walk up 18 through a tunnel of spectators.

Magical. That's what St. Andrews is to all lovers of golf or Scotland or both. And on each succeeding trip, more of its mystery and history unfolds for you. There is a mystique, an aura, no other place possesses.

Most visitors are golfers, and that's the only passport you need to enter the Kingdom of Fife. Shopkeepers, publicans, hoteliers and restaurateurs make you feel as a resident, even if only temporary.

There is the lasting presence of the Old Course and its attendant sisters, all of which should be played by visitors, but seldom are. They are grand links. There is the overpowering sense of history of golf as we know it, dating back to the 14th century, at least. There are the historical edifices that remind visitors the town once was a religious center, and still is a world-renowned seat of learning. The graveyard is more than that, it is a shrine.

When the final link with the glories of the past died, a great void was created in the heroic form of Laurie Auchterlonie — master clubmaker, historian, collector, and a player of note who detested the pressures of competition. He once shot 59 at Crail, up the road.

His father before him had won an Open and his uncle a U.S. Open, and this great man in heart and stature had seen the heroes play. "My father didn't compete often, but he was the best," Laurie would reminisce.

"He had to give Jimmy strokes before they played a match." Jimmy? "James Braid," Laurie would say in a wondering tone. Did he think we all knew him as Jimmy? During that 1984 Open my wife and I scoured the town for history. Browsing in book, art or golf shops we inevitably unearthed something interesting. I would take these bits back to Laurie each evening in his flat, where he was recuperating from an illness, and discuss them. He sorted out the fact from fiction.

One day we played the Jubilee Course, and duly reported to Laurie. "And how did ye like it?" he inquired. I told him I enjoyed it as much as any of the courses there. "I'm happy to hear that," he said. "My father designed it." You can imagine my mental state upon learning that.

Seeing the town and course without 70,000 spectators is a shock. It is so clearly defined. But once I saw it under ephemerally eerie circumstances.

During March several years ago a group of pilgrims from America visited St. Andrews when the town and golf courses were under two inches of snow. We were told it's a rarity that occurs maybe every 100 years. It was the most beautiful sight we had ever seen. Not one of us had a camera. A group of youngsters was in the 18th fairway trying to build a snowman with little success, it being their first.

I have a painting of this snow scene, one of four St. Andrews landscapes, on the wall of my totally golf-oriented home in Pinehurst, North Carolina. Old Tom and Laurie Auchterlonie also grace the collection.

Only once did I encounter a person who was disappointed by his visit to St. Andrews. He was a Southern Californian, a breed apart, and he made continuous disparaging remarks about the Old Course. After six holes I told him what I thought about his total insensitiveness to the hallowed surroundings and walked off the course. I felt good about that all day.

That night Auchterlonie chided me. "Ye should have told him to play through. Ye paid for the round and ye should hae finished." Spoken like a true Scot, and I love 'em all.

♦

"Magical. That's what St. Andrews is to all lovers of golf or Scotland or both."

55

♦

As a golf historian and essayist, Herb Wind has no equals. A graduate of Yale and Cambridge, he's best known for writing golf essays during his years at The New Yorker *(1948-1954 and 1962-1990) and* Sports Illustrated *(1954-1960) and for authoring more than a dozen golf books, including* The Story of American Golf *and bestsellers with Gene Sarazen, Ben Hogan and Jack Nicklaus. Wind has been known to excel on the golf course, too; he has been a member of the R & A for nearly 40 years and competed in the 1950 British Amateur over the Old Course.*

EYEWITNESS RECOLLECTIONS OF WORLD-CLASS GOLF

by Herbert Warren Wind

My life has been made considerably richer by my good fortune in being able to visit St. Andrews at fairly frequent intervals. I went there first in the spring of 1938, when I was doing some graduate work in England. A Scottish friend suggested that we drive up to the "auld grey toun" the first weekend in June and take in the Walker Cup, the 10th in the series of biennial meetings between Great Britain-Ireland and the United States that had begun in 1922. A fairly large number of talented American amateurs, headed by Bobby Jones, had come into their own during this period, and our teams had swept the first nine matches.

My friend and I arrived at St. Andrews a little before noon on the Friday when the teams were completing the first 18 holes of the four 36-hole foursomes matches. I had never seen a course like the Old Course. As you know, it is laid out over a narrow, treeless peninsula that noses into a small bay off the North Sea. The first seven holes march in single file to the north; the next four perform the celebrated clockwise loop; and the last seven march back in single file to the town. On a sunny day the towers of St. Andrews' handsome medieval buildings — including the spires of St. Andrews University, which was founded in the 15th century — glint and glow in the distance. More than one visitor has compared the thrill of playing the last seven holes of the Old Course to the feeling that must have overcome travelers in the Middle Ages as they closed in on Camelot.

In 1938 my friend and I gradually got our bearing. We decided that in the afternoon we would start by watching the first of the four foursomes matches: Johnny Fischer and Charlie Kocsis were 3-up at lunch on Harry Bentley, the popular English veteran, and James Bruen, the brawny 18-year-old Irishman, who could bust the ball out of sight. On the third hole, a drive-and-pitch par 4 to one of the Old Course's fast and subtly breaking greens, the American pair had a chance to bolster its lead if Fischer could get down the 12-foot birdie putt that Kocsis' pitch had set up. Fischer left the ball about a foot short of the cup. Displeased with himself, he

One of the trademarks of the Old Course is that there are seven double greens. These enormous greens have two holes, one used by golfers on the outgoing loop and the other used by those heading inward. Shown here is the green serving the fifth and 13th holes. More than 50,000 square feet in size, it is recognized as the "world's largest green."

walked to the ball and quickly tapped it in. In doing this he had played out of turn — it had been Kocsis' turn to play. Young Bruen excitedly called the referee's attention to this infraction of the rules and claimed that the hole belonged to Great Britain-Ireland. At this point Bentley calmly intervened. He told the referee that the hole had been halved — he had conceded the Americans' short putt. He did not want this international match to be marred by some inappropriate technicality.

We spent the rest of the afternoon popping from one foursomes match to another. The British play foursomes regularly and they are skilled at it. At the close of the day's play, the match between Bentley-and-Bruen and Fischer-and-Kocsis ended, fittingly, in a tie. Down the stretch the British pair, trailing by two holes with three to play, won the 16th, and on the very testing 17th they at length squared the match when Bentley holed for a birdie from 45 feet. They barely missed winning the 18th. In those days no half-points were awarded in a halved match in Walker Cup play. Accordingly, at the end of play on the first day, the score was Great Britain-Ireland 2, United States 1.

On the second (and last) day, a perfect one for golf since just enough wind was abroad to make things interesting, the home team, playing with increased confidence, won five of the eight 36-hole singles matches. The three American winners were Fischer, Marvin "Bud" Ward and Charlie Yates, who two weeks before the Walker Cup match had carried off the British Amateur Championship at Troon. Ward shot a 67 in the morning en route to winning his match, 12 & 11; Fischer, 4-down at lunch, ripped off six consecutive 3s midway through the afternoon to take command of his match; and Yates got his nose out in front of Bruen and vigilantly nullified the Irishman's tremendous hitting. The final score of the team match was Great Britain-Ireland 7, United States 4.

The presentation ceremonies were held on the steps of the stately sandstone clubhouse of the Royal and Ancient Golf Club. The jubilant Scottish throng was spread out over the adjoining first and 18th fairways. They cheered the American players. They liked their friendliness and the way

The ominous Road Hole Bunker, one of the most famous in golf, guards the left side of the 17th green. Not only does it regularly attract approach shots, it's been known to swallow up errant putts from championship-caliber golfers.

The starter's box is adjacent to the first tee.

they went about playing golf. They let the British-Irish team know how deeply they appreciated its resolution in at last gaining possession of the Walker Cup after nine straight defeats. When the formal program was concluded, no one wanted to leave. The crowd kept calling for the Scottish players, the other home-team favorites, and individual American players, foremostly Yates, whose Georgia accent and easy banter had gone down so well at St. Andrews and also with the galleries at Troon during the British Amateur. Yates talked things over briefly with Gordon Peters, a Scottish member of the winning team, who had taught him the old Scottish air, "Just A Wee Doch and Dorris." Yates and Peters then led the delighted thousands in a couple of spirited choruses of that old favorite. It turned out to be the perfect note on which to end a rare occasion.

Anyone who was present at the closing ceremonies of the 1938 Walker Cup match never forgot it. For me it was the first international sports event I attended where the level of performance was exceedingly high and where the spectators as well as the players were caught up in the wonderful spirit that sports can engender. That is why I returned to St. Andrews as often as I could whenever an event of some consequence was held there. Let me briefly describe my subsequent visits.

In the spring of 1950 I was on hand for the first British Amateur Championship to be held at St. Andrews since the close of the Second World War. A record number of golfers — 324 — entered the event. Golfers from every part of the globe regarded this championship at St. Andrews as *the* occasion to get together with old friends they hadn't seen for far too long. In retrospect, the new batch of long-hitting young Americans dominated the play, with Frank Stranahan defeating Dick Chapman in the 36-hole final. (Bing Crosby was in the starting field. He drew huge crowds and showed himself to be an accomplished player. He birdied two of the first three holes.)

During the week I had a chance to talk with Bernard Darwin, the noted British golf writer, for the first time since 1939. I did some research in the club's wonderful library. I got to meet Stewart Lawson, a resident of St. Andrews, who probably knew more about the rules of golf than anyone else in the post war world. I also got to know Sir Guy Campbell, the prominent golf historian. I happened to ask him where the old St. Andrews caddies positioned themselves down the first fairway back in 1922 when the Prince of Wales, the incoming R & A captain, drove himself into office. You see, the caddie who retrieves the new captain's tee shot and returns the ball to him traditionally receives a gold sovereign. Sir Guy smiled and replied, "I'm afraid they stood disloyally close."

My work allowed me to be at St. Andrews in 1955 when, for the first time since 1938, the Walker Cup was again held there. Bill Campbell served as the captain of a U.S. team on which, I believe, none of our players except Campbell himself had ever played in Britain. On the first day, when the foursomes were held, Campbell kept himself out of the lineup. He felt he could contribute more by talking with the players and cheering them on. The Americans swept the four foursomes. In the singles the following day, Campbell went with the same eight players. With Harvie Ward and Billy Joe Patton leading the way, the American team added six of the eight singles to complete a remarkable 10-2 victory.

American participation in the Open Championship got off to a gradual start. Back in 1946, Sam Snead had flown to Scotland on the relative eve of the 1946 Championship, which was held at St. Andrews. Despite the cold wind and rain off the North Sea, Sam won by four strokes. But he didn't bother to defend his title. At that time, few of our touring pros were interested in going over for the Open. The prize money in Britain was minimal. They could do much better at home playing the PGA's expanding summer tour. In 1953, Ben Hogan, after winning the Masters and our Open with the finest golf of his career, had the good sense to send in his entry for the Open, scheduled for Carnoustie that summer. Nipping the ball off the very firm turf like the old Scottish golfers had done, Hogan's play from tee to green was practically flawless, and he won the championship by

four strokes. He did not return to defend his title either.

It was Arnold Palmer who made it practically compulsory for the top American pros to be on hand for the Open. In 1960, after carrying off the Masters and our Open, he was one of the few Americans in the starting field at St. Andrews when the centenary of

the Open was celebrated. Palmer played courageously through several violent storms and made a brave closing rush, but Kel Nagle, of Australia, came through with some wonderful golf down the stretch and edged out Palmer by a stroke. I happened to be standing near Palmer outside the clubhouse just before Nagle holed the

*A surprise to many is that the R & A owns neither the Old
Course nor the five adjoining courses, but rather shares in
the management of the publicly owned links.*

This stone bridge provides golfers with a route over the Swilken Burn after they tee off on the 18th hole of the Old Course. Dating to the 12th century, the bridge originally provided a crossing for townsfolk venturing out to the Eden River. In recent times, the bridge has served virtually every famous golf champion, from Allan Robertson and Tom Morris in the mid-19th century to current stars such as Seve Ballesteros and Nick Faldo.

winning putt on the 18th green. When Arnold walked past me on his way into the clubhouse, I said to him, "You played wonderful golf." He shook his head and replied, "It wasn't good enough." He then headed for the players' changing room to clean out his locker.

The following summer, Palmer returned to win the Open at Royal Birkdale under brutal conditions. With his tremendous raw strength, he was able to tear his ball out of seemingly unplayable lies in the deep, dense rough on the last two rounds and to edge out Dai Rees, of Wales, by a stroke. He successfully defended his title at Troon, where he finished six strokes ahead of the runner-up, Nagle, and 13 shots ahead of the third-place finishers.

In three short years, Palmer, with his attacking golf and rare charisma, had restored the Open to its former place in the sun. From that year on, every forward-looking professional in the world found a way to be in the starting field in July at St. Andrews and the other venues.

One year after Palmer had made his debut in the Open in 1960, I found myself in St. Andrews in a novel capacity. I was one of the persons who had a hand in devising the format of "Shell's Wonderful World of Golf," the long-running series of television shows in which the top American professionals met the top foreign professionals on the best courses in the world. After filming the first two matches — Byron Nelson vs. Gene Littler at Pine Valley, and Jay Hebert vs. Flory Van Donck of Belgium at St. Cloud, outside Paris — we went up to St.

Andrews where Gene Sarazen, the host of the series, played a slightly younger maestro, Henry Cotton of England.

They met on a cold, gray day in August when heavy, twisting winds ripped across the Old Course. By the time Sarazen and Cotton had reached the loop, a chilling rain caused a suspension of play. Around noon, someone brought out sandwiches and

tea for the players and the camera crews. Shortly after play was resumed, the winds began to diminish in force, the rain gradually stopped, the sky brightened, and the two venerable champions were heading back to town with a light breeze at their backs. Cotton began to hit the ball like Cotton. Sarazen, as shrewd as ever, began to use his 3-wood off the tees — he could control the ball better with it. The two

"My life has been made considerably richer by my good fortune in being able to visit St. Andrews at fairly frequent intervals."

— Herbert Warren Wind

Golfers playing the par-3 11th, or High Hole (In), are faced with several challenges. The steeply sloping green is protected at the front by the deep Strath and Hill bunkers. Club selection varies from long iron to wedge, depending on wind strength and direction. Compounding these challenges is the fact that the double green serves the seventh, or High Hole (Out), and that the line of play on the seventh hole crosses in front of those playing the 11th. This hole got the best of 19-year-old Bobby Jones, playing in the third round of the 1921 Open Championship. After Jones drove into Hill Bunker and made several unsuccessful attempts to get out, he reportedly picked up his ball and went to the next tee in disgust. Later realizing that a bad temper had no place on the golf course, he not only apologized for his brashness, but became an advocate of good sportsmanship and won the hearts of St. Andreans.

men began to play one handsome shot after another.

The match reached its climax on the famous 17th hole, which then measured 466 yards from the back tee to the well-protected green. Sarazen got home with a 3-wood off the tee and a perfect 4-wood that ended up at the extreme back of the green some 60 feet past the flag. He stroked the dangerous putt confidently. The ball held its line and at length expired inches from the cup. After Cotton had two-putted from 25 feet for a 5, Sarazen tapped in his tiny putt for his 4 to go ahead by a stroke. The two champions halved the 18th with 4s. A day that seemed headed for disaster ended with one of the most arresting matches in the extended Shell series safely in the can.

Nineteen sixty-three was a Walker Cup year. The match was played at Turnberry on the west coast of Scotland, and Billy Joe Patton provided the spark once again, as the Americans rallied on the second day to win the match, 12 - 8. A week or so later, the British Amateur got under way at St. Andrews.

The championship turned out to be a rather quiet one, but I look back at it fondly. First, it was won by a best-of-the-breed young Englishman, Michael Lunt, who took the club back perfectly and, when he didn't hurry his tempo at the top of his backswing, could hit the ball past most profes-

Mother Nature makes her presence known on the links, from bluebells blowing in the wind to encounters with a weasel.

sionals. Near the end of the week, when only the four semifinalists remained on the scene, St. Andrews was too quiet to be restful. In one bracket Dr. Ed Updegraff, from Tucson, lost to Lunt on the last green. Lunt was expected to have little trouble the next day in the 36-hole final match against John Blackwell, a wealthy middle-aged schoolmaster who taught at one of England's renowned "public schools." Before a big match, Blackwell, a high-strung, silver-haired chap, tried to keep himself calm and relaxed by playing Broadway show tunes on the record player in his automobile. Lunt was expected to make short work of him. He was in top form on the morning round but could make little headway against an inspired opponent. After lunch, instead of cracking, Blackwell, cheerfully humming to himself a medley of Rogers and Hart show tunes, continued to hit one crisp shot after another. Down the stretch, however, he missed a couple of putts, and Lunt closed out the match, 2 & 1.

I wasn't on hand at St. Andrews in 1964 when Tony Lema, on his first trip to Britain to play in the Open, did not allow himself sufficient time to prepare properly for the rigors of linksland golf. Somehow or other, he played four brilliant rounds in very stormy weather and finished five strokes ahead of Jack Nicklaus, the runner-up.

Jack had broken through in the Open in 1966 at Muirfield. The next 14 years he finished sixth or better in the championship. Two of those years, 1970 and 1978, he won it, both times at St. Andrews. In 1978, when the

64

Open was played during what was regarded in Scotland as a heat wave, Jack edged out his principal threat, Simon Owen of New Zealand, by 2 strokes.

In 1970, it had been quite different. On the 72nd green, Doug Sanders, a Georgian who had moved to Texas, missed a slippery $3^1/_2$-foot putt for his par. This gave Jack an unexpected reprieve. For the only time in history, a playoff in the Open at St. Andrews was decided on a Sunday. No tickets were required. The townspeople poured onto the Old Course with their youngsters and their dogs. Throughout the afternoon no baby fussed or cried and no dog barked. With five holes to play, Nicklaus led by 4 strokes. Sanders got two of them back with birdies on the 14th and 15th. He picked up another stroke when Nicklaus three-putted the 16th. Two great 4s on the 17th. On the 350-yard 18th, with a turbulent wind at the players' backs, Sanders had his birdie 3 all the way: his drive ended up just short of the green, his run-up inches from the cup. Nicklaus' drive had bounded over the green and finished in the tangled rough behind it. He played a delicate recovery shot with his wedge. The ball trickled down the fast green and stopped 7 feet or so above the hole. For a moment it looked as if he had tapped his putt just to the right of the cup, but the ball caught the corner and dropped. That was it. Nicklaus tossed his putter high in the air, and, in his jubilation, almost forgot that he had. Then the two men collapsed on each other's shoulders.

The 23rd Walker Cup match took place at St. Andrews in late May 1971,

Bluebells in the dunes.

Thistles in the rough. Admired by many as the Scottish national flower, the thistle plant is often cursed by golfers...especially when it interferes with one's backswing!

Many visitors are unaware that there is no one "official" clubhouse for the golf courses at St. Andrews. Although the Royal and Ancient Golf Club is the most prominent, several other clubs claim the town's golf courses as their home courses: the St. Andrews Golf Club, home club to 19th-century champions Allan Robertson and Old Tom and Young Tom Morris; the New Club, which claims Bobby Jones and Arnold Palmer as honorary members; and St. Rule and St. Regulus, both ladies' clubs.

and, thank goodness, I was on hand. The British-Irish team still hadn't won the cup since that glorious weekend in 1938. (It had tied the 1965 match at the Five Farms course of the Baltimore Country Club, but that had hurt more than the one-sided defeats. With eight singles remaining to be played on the second afternoon, the visitors needed to take just two of them to win the match.) Michael Bonallack, captaining the team for the second time, brought his players into the 1971 match in a relaxed and confident frame of mind. In the morning of the first day, the British-Irish swept the four foursomes, all of them hard-fought. The American team struck back in the afternoon. It took six of the eight singles and halved another. The margin of victory in four of those matches was one hole. In their singles match, Bill Hyndman and Roddy Carr, the son of Joe Carr, the best of all the talented Irish amateurs, finished all even. The score at the end of the first day: United States 6½, Great Britain-Ireland 5½.

Going into the second day, the general feeling was that the American team would probably win. It had too many guns. Bill Campbell, who had been a member of six Walker Cup teams, was on hand once again, but the team was largely made up of confident young players who were attending warm-weather colleges on golf scholarships. After the Americans had solidified their slim lead by taking 2½ of the 4 points in the foursomes on the morning of the second day, the general feeling, as I remember it, was that the team match was as good as over. Bonallack, in any

event, had placed himself in the top singles match in the afternoon in the hope that if he managed to outplay the tough and talented Lanny Wadkins, it might rouse his teammates to rise to the occasion. Bonallack played wonderfully aggressive golf, but Wadkins closed him out on the 17th green. At just about that time, though, there was an unexpected turn of events: the players on the home team began to do things. Warren Humphreys, a gifted young player who had never fulfilled his promise, started to

Golf at St. Andrews used to be free. A modest green fee was first imposed for visitors in 1913 and for residents in 1946.

Waiting to tee off on the eighth hole of the New Course, a 481-yard par 5, that shares a fairway with the 12th.

The Old Course is a wind-swept links course, highlighted with endless undulations and strategically placed bunkers instead of the water hazards and trees typical of inland courses. The lone place that water affects play is on the first hole, where the Swilken Burn meanders across the front of the green. Rather than facing trees on the horizon — there are only three small ones on the entire course — golfers are confronted with the St. Andrews skyline on the finishing holes. In the foreground of this 1961 painting, golfers putt on the then-parched 15th green.

outdrive the powerful Steve Melnyk and took control of their match by holing two sinuous birdie putts of over 30 feet on the 15th and 16th. He then closed out their match on the 17th. Roddy Carr produced some excellent golf on the second nine and went on to win his match with Jim Simons, 2-up, when he holed a 20-foot birdie putt on the home green. On an out-and-back course like St. Andrews, there was no way for the spectators to move deftly around, and besides, there were no scoreboards set up around the course.

As the afternoon wore on, most of the experienced American golf-watchers gathered midway down the right side of the 17th fairway where they could take in the play on that historically decisive hole and, with the aid of binoculars, see what was taking place on the 18th. In the end, the player who won the competition for the British-Irish team was David Marsh, a young English physician. On the 17th, all even with Bill Hyndman in the seventh singles, he was informed that the home team needed to win one more point to win the match. (By this time, Tom Kite had defeated Geoff Marks in the last singles.) Marsh laced a long tee-shot down the fairway. He followed it with a 3-iron that covered the flag all the way and finished about 14 feet from it. That remarkable shot won the Walker Cup. Marsh carefully two-putted the 17th for a birdie 4 to go 1-up. He had his par all the way on the 18th. Great Britain-Ireland 13, United States 11.

A watercolor study depicting the eighth green of the New Course.

*The Old Course got its name in the early
1890s when the New Course was established.*

David Honeyman was greenkeeper for 35 years until his death in 1903. His mentor was Old Tom Morris, whose frequent recommendations of "mair saund" (more sand topdressing) kept the greens in playable condition.

Walter Woods, links supervisor, oversees the upkeep of all six St. Andrews golf courses. Through careful use of modern fertilizers and underground irrigation systems, he strives to maintain the traditional character of the links.

Pandemonium erupted.

The celebrating lasted into the wee small hours. I made the rounds with an old friend, Fred Tupper, a Vermonter who lived in London and covered many of the important international sports events for *The New York Times*. We had a wonderful visit with the American players and the USGA contingent. They were delighted that the British-Irish team had recaptured the cup after 33 years in the wilderness. That night at the various parties we joined our English, Scottish and Irish friends in celebrating the joyous occasion. Gerald Micklem, an old and admirable friend who had played in four Walker Cup matches and twice captained the British-Irish team, said to us emotionally, "I'm happy that I have lived to see this day." We walked back to our hotel shortly after midnight. On our way across the 18th and first fairways we watched some youthful celebrators jump into the waters of the Swilcan Burn in front of the first green.

I returned to St. Andrews on two subsequent occasions. In 1981, Ben Crenshaw and I led a group of American golfers who were interested in golf course architecture. We toured some of the renowned courses in Scotland and England and played the Old Course on a mild and sunny day. That evening, we had drinks in the R & A clubhouse.

My last visit to St. Andrews came in 1984. By that time, Tom Watson had won the Open five times — at Carnoustie in 1975, Turnberry in 1977, Muirfield in 1980, Troon in 1982 and Birkdale in 1983. He was

Long gone are the days when greenkeepers had to rely on grazing livestock to keep the turf trimmed.

Motorized triplex mowers now perform tasks once delegated to roaming sheep and workers with hand-held scythes. Here, a worker hoses off his equipment.

TOURISM BOOMS WITH THE ARRIVAL OF THE RAILWAY

In 1847, St. Andrews first became accessible by rail. No longer did travelers have to rely entirely on dusty carriage paths and rough sea passages. Those destined for St. Andrews rode the train to the nearby town of Leuchars and traveled the remaining four miles by horse-drawn coach. Over the next five years, the St. Andrews Railway was constructed, enabling passengers to ride all the way from Leuchars to the Links Station — located on the present site of the Old Course Hotel. By the 1880s, more track was laid and a new station opened in town. The Links Station became a freight depot. Today the stationmaster's house is home to the popular Jigger Inn.

When the elaborate railroad bridge spanning the Firth of Forth opened in 1890, St. Andrews became easily accessible to Edinburgh. This resulted in an onslaught of tourists as golfers and sea bathers descended on the town. By World War II, though, there was a noticeable decline in passenger train usage as automobile travel increased. Service to St. Andrews was abandoned in 1969, but travelers still have easy bus or auto access to the stations in Edinburgh, Dundee, and Leuchars.

74

The railroad once paralleled the incoming holes of the Old Course. This scene is from the 1930s.

"One ritual at St. Andrews is the closing of the Old Course on Sunday to give it a rest…"

— *John Hopkins*

out to win the championship a sixth time and tie the record Harry Vardon had set in 1914. Tom had an excellent chance to do this. Moving down the stretch on the fourth round, he led Seve Ballesteros, the closest contender, by a stroke.

Ballesteros was playing in the twosome just in front of Watson. After hooking a wild drive into tall, thick rough many yards off the 17th fairway, Ballesteros made one of his seemingly impossible recovery shots. He followed by holing a subtly breaking putt for his 4. Watson took in all of this. He had hit a garish slice off the tee, but his ball had finished on the fairway a few yards short of the out-of-bounds territory. Knowing Ballesteros made his 4, Watson had no alternative but to go for the green on his second — no small order in the wicked left-to-right wind that had suddenly kicked up. The wind got hold of Watson's thinly hit sliced fairway wood. It shoved the ball far to the right and, at length, onto the paved road that runs below the right edge of the green. The ball ended up about a foot from the stone wall on the far side of the road. The road plays as a hazard: You cannot sole your club on it. Watson had to improvise a way to hack the ball away from the wall, which he did. He then got down in a chip and two putts for a 6. It was a sad way to lose a major championship, but, as Watson appreciated, he hadn't played well enough to win it.

Some time later, I saw a slow-motion film that showed what had happened to Watson's second. The ball did not hit one of the fairly large stones

in the wall as many thought. It actually hit the relatively soft clay between the stones, dropped down almost meekly, and stayed where it landed.

I have purposely left out of order — saved for last — the visit to St. Andrews that meant the most to me. There are some stretches in October when it is just too cold to play golf in St. Andrews, but in the second week of October 1958 the "auld grey toun" was thick with golfers from Argentina, Iceland, Malaya, and 25 other nations around the world. In late June that year, delegates from the golf associations of most of those countries had met in Washington at the invitation of the USGA and the R & A. They formed the World Amateur Golf Council, and arranged for four-man teams from the member nations to assemble in St. Andrews in October to participate in the first World Amateur Team Championship for the Eisenhower Trophy. The format for the competition could have hardly been improved. On each of the four days, each country would arrive at its score by adding up the three lowest scores of its four players. Each country's grand total for the 72 holes was the sum of its daily three-man totals. The winner at St. Andrews was Australia. Australia and the United States had finished with total of 918, one stroke lower than Great Britain and Ireland. In the 18-hole playoff, Australia edged out the United States, 222 - 224. This biennial competition, by the way, is alive and well.

Robert Tyre Jones Jr., the immortal Bobby, came to St. Andrews that autumn as the captain of the

U.S. team. (Jones had made his first visit to St. Andrews 37 years before, when he made his debut in the Open Championship.) He watched the practice rounds of the four-man American team — Charlie Coe, Billy Joe Patton, Dr. Bud Taylor and Bill Hyndman — in the electric cart he brought over with him. He used the cart to get to the various official functions in the evening. On Thursday night, the town of St. Andrews seized the opportunity to make Jones an Honorary Burgess of the Borough — the first American to be honored since Benjamin Franklin 199 years before. The ceremony took place in Younger Hall, the largest auditorium in town. Seventeen hundred fervent St. Andreans crammed it to the rafters, literally.

Jones spoke without notes that evening. (He ripped them up after listening to the Town Provost's rather extraordinary words of welcome.) The occasion and the warmth of his audience fired Jones to a high pitch of eloquence. I remember what he said of the Old Course, "The more you study it, the more you love it, and the more you love it, the more you study it." He also said, "I could take out of my life everything except my experiences at St. Andrews and I would still have a rich, full life." At the end of his talk, Jones was helped from the stage to his golf cart, and as he directed it down the center aisle, the whole hall suddenly burst into the old Scottish song, "Will Ye No' Come Back Again?" It came pouring out with all the wild, overwhelming emotion of a pibroch (a form of bagpipe music) wailing in some lonesome glen.

NINETY-NINE HOLES OF GOLF

Mention St. Andrews to anyone who hasn't been there and he or she most likely will conjure up images of the windswept Old Course and the imposing clubhouse of the Royal and Ancient Golf Club. What most fail to realize is that R & A members own a clubhouse, not a golf course, and that the Old Course is merely a portion of one of the world's largest public golf facilities.

Included on the 650 acres at the town's western edge are five 18-hole courses (Old, New, Eden, Jubilee and Strathtyrum), a nine-hole beginner's course (Balgove), an enormous putting course (The Himalayas), a spacious new clubhouse and a state-of-the-art practice complex. All are controlled by the St. Andrews Links Trust, which was created by an Act of Parliament in 1974 after Scotland's local governments were restructured. The trust is required to "maintain the Links as a public park and place of public resort and recreation for the residents of the town of St. Andrews."

The Old Course is the most famous and has been played on for more than 500 years. Once consisting of 22 holes, it was shortened to 18 in the mid-18th century. It was the only course in town until the New Course opened in 1895. Of all the courses, the New is ranked second to the Old in terms of difficulty. The Jubilee Course opened in 1897, the year of Queen Victoria's Diamond Jubilee. Although at 6,805 yards, the Jubilee is the longest of the courses, it can be played in a 5,674-yard, par-69 configuration called the Bronze Course.

The remaining three courses start conveniently near the Eden Information Centre and the new Golf Practice Centre, with its floodlit areas and covered bays. The Eden Course originally dates to 1914, but was extensively revamped in 1988. The Balgove has nine short holes for beginners and children. The newest course, the Strathtyrum, was designed by Donald Steel to challenge the average golfer. It opened in 1993.

In 1995, visitors were finally provided with a proper clubhouse for changing and dining. Located behind the 18th green of the New Course, it serves golfers at the adjoining New and Jubilee courses, and is a short shuttle from the first hole of the Old Course. (Locals traditionally belong to and utilize the facilities at the various golf clubs which neighbor the links.)

Tee times are allocated by a strict — and often confusing — set of guidelines. There are more than 75,000 golfing visitors to St. Andrews each year, and most want to play the fabled Old Course. Reservations can be obtained by applying in advance, by purchasing a golf "package" from a travel agent or through a lottery known as the "daily ballot." In the ballot, golfers submit their names in the morning for play the following day, and await the posting of successful applicants in the afternoon. The regulations provide for lower green fees and certain advantages in the ballot for residents and members of the R & A.

A Window on Golf

by Doreen Mould

As a great-granddaughter of the legendary Tom Morris (1821-1908), Doreen "Bunty" Mould is responsible for keeping his legacy alive. Like many of Old Tom's descendants, she has a fondness for golf. She and her husband currently live a short ride down the seacoast from St. Andrews.

I guess I'm sort of a link to an earlier time of golf in St. Andrews, for I own the property at numbers 7 and 8 The Links, where Tom Morris lived and operated his golf shop in his later years. I inherited it in 1935 from my widowed mother, Ellen Hunter, who had died in London, where we were living at the time. Old Tom was my father's grandfather, and I had heard much about his reputation as the "grand old man of golf" while growing up.

In 1938, I moved into the house, with its excellent view of the Old Course's finishing hole. The front door is only about 60 feet from the edge of the green! Old Tom's shop, which still exists today, is on the ground floor and the living quarters are upstairs (see page 82). It's no wonder the old magazines wrote how he used to lean out of the window to chat with those below and to command the local boys not to practice putting on the 18th green; you literally have a front-row seat for all the goings-on.

I have seen many great golfing events from this window, including many Open Championships and the marvelous Walker Cup of 1938. The worst thing I can remember was standing at the window while listening on the "wireless"

to Mr. Chamberlain declaring that Britain was at war with Germany. I felt devastated, aware that our lives and the world would be changed forever. I was a newlywed; my husband, Jack, was in the Royal Air Force and we would spend the next six years away from St. Andrews. He remained in the RAF and retired as a Wing Commander in 1962.

Although the front of my building is right on the road where there is constant activity during the warmer months, there is a peaceful garden in the rear where we can relax. In my younger days, we could hear the sounds of machinery from Forgan's golf club factory next door. That was a minor annoyance we learned to ignore. The greatest hazard was, and still is, the occasional errant golf ball on the 18th that comes crashing through one of the windows.

After Old Tom died in 1908, several family members, including my father, operated the golf shop for about 20 years. In 1927, there was an offer by a group of Americans who wished to buy the house and turn it into a club. My father wisely turned it down. He eventually rented out the shop to nonfamily members, a situation that still exists today. Until recently, I maintained a directorship position in the business. Now there is a long-term lease that will keep the Tom Morris name alive in St. Andrews.

Old Tom Morris — clubmaker, ballmaker, caddie, golf course designer, greenkeeper, four-time Open champion — poses on the links above the West Sands.

80

Only one of Old Tom's three children, Elizabeth, had children. Her husband, James Hunter, was a wood merchant in Prestwick. Their son, William Bruce Hunter, is shown with his grandfather, circa 1881 (right), and as a young man (above). William's daughter is Doreen Mould.

◆

Although golf had been played for centuries, the first professional golfers didn't appear until the mid-1800s. Among the first were Tom and Tommy Morris, Allan Robertson, Willie Park (Sr. and Jr.), Willie and Jamie Dunn, and Andrew and David Strath.

◆

The story of Tom Morris Jr. – also known as Young Tom or Tommy – is one of the most poignant in golf. He was acknowledged as the greatest golfer of his time, and won the Open three times in succession, from 1868-1870, thus retiring the championship belt displayed in this painting. There was no championship the following year, and in 1872 Morris became the first winner of the silver claret jug still symbolic of the competition. In the fall of 1875, Tommy and his father were playing a match against Open champions and brothers Willie and Mungo Park in North Berwick, when a telegram arrived informing them that Tommy's pregnant wife was critically ill. The Morrises left immediately for St. Andrews, but while they were enroute, they received another message that both mother and child died during childbirth. To add further sadness to the story, Young Tom died three months later on Christmas Day. Legend says that the 24-year-old hero died of a broken heart; actually, he suffered from a burst blood vessel. Today, thousands of golfers pay tribute to Young Tom at his grave in the town's cemetery (see page 32).

82

This stone building opposite the 18th green has been associated with Tom Morris since he opened his shop there in 1866. Originally a one-story building, he later added the second floor and lived there until his death in 1908. The retail shop on the ground floor still carries his name today. Prior to Morris, other craftsmen had their clubmaking shops on the site: Hugh Philp, Robert Forgan and G.D. Brown.

One of the best places to view the finish of the Open Championship is the second-floor parlor in Old Tom's house. The building is cared for today by his great-granddaughter, Doreen Mould, shown here in conversation with her husband, Wing Commander Jack Mould (left), and co-author Mort Olman.

◆

"I have been told that Old Tom and Young Tom had a cult following in the 1860s and '70s, just as The Beatles had a century later."

— Doreen Mould

◆

84

In the winter of 1902, the R & A commissioned artist Sir George Reid, president of the Royal Scottish Academy, to paint a formal portrait of Old Tom. Here, the legendary golfer is shown arriving for a sitting in Edinburgh in an early automobile along with his granddaughter and Mrs. P.G. Tait (see letter on following page). Today the painting hangs prominently in the Big Room of the R & A clubhouse. (In 1903, the painting was reproduced in a limited quantity of black-and-white photogravures.)

♦

Old Tom competed in every Open Championship
from its inception in 1860 through 1896.

♦

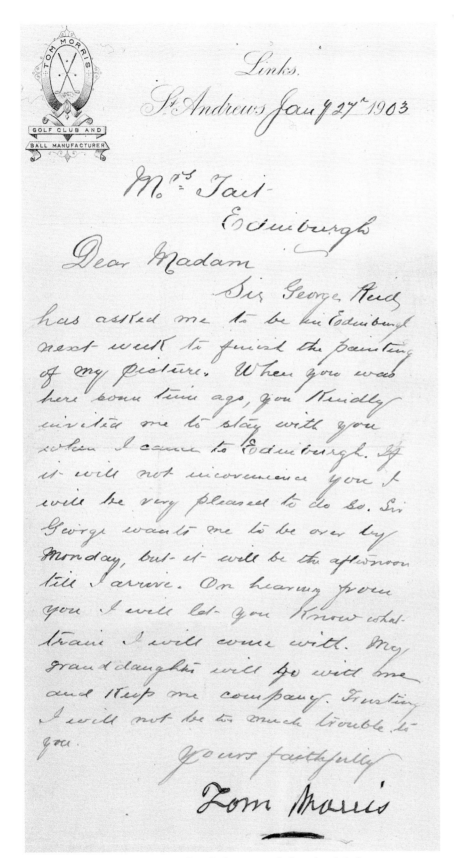

January 27, 1903

Mrs. Tait - Edinburgh

Dear Madam:

    Sir George Reid has asked me to be in Edinburgh next week to finish the painting of my picture. When you was here some time ago, you kindly invited me to stay with you when I came to Edinburgh. If it will not inconvenience you, I will be very pleased to do so. Sir George wants me to be over by Monday, but it will be the afternoon till I arrive. On hearing from you, I will let you know what train I will come with. My Granddaughter will go with me and keep me company. Trusting I will not be too much trouble to you.

        Yours faithfully,
        Tom Morris

Old Tom sent this letter regarding lodging in Edinburgh while his portrait was being completed. It is addressed to Mrs. Tait, mother of the famous golfer Freddie Tait. The letter, signed by Morris, probably was written by his granddaughter.

Allan Robertson, of St. Andrews, was golf's first superstar.

The Greatest Player Never to Win the Open

At the time of his death in 1859, Allan Robertson was heralded as the best golfer the game had ever known. Just as Arnold Palmer became known by just his nickname "Arnie" in the 1960s, Robertson was known just as "Allan." He was born into a family of ballmakers and caddies in St. Andrews in 1815. The Robertsons had made feather balls by hand since at least the early 1700s. While other makers imprinted balls with their last names, Robertson just stamped "ALLAN" in capital letters on his golf balls.

Allan was one of the game's first professionals. When not making balls in the 1840s and '50s, he would compete in money matches, often partnered with his apprentice, Tom Morris, who was six years younger. During this period, Allan rarely lost. He was the first to master the use of an iron-headed club with the delicate feather ball for other than trouble shots. He learned to make delicate approach shots with his favorite iron, which he nicknamed "the frying pan."

In 1848, Robertson and Morris reportedly had a falling-out and terminated their relationship. Legend has it that Allan was furious when he learned that Morris was playing with the just developed gutty ball. The gutty, molded from rubber-like gutta-percha, was a low-cost alternative to the expensive feather ball, and Allan vehemently opposed its use. He saw the gutty as a threat to his ballmaking business. After an argument, the two parted ways, and Morris opened his own shop, where he produced both types of balls. By the early 1850s, Allan began to produce — and use — the new ball. In 1858, it was with the gutty that he became the first to break 80 over the St. Andrews links. That round occurred a few months before his death, and a little more than a year before the first Open was contested. If the professionals of the 1850s had ever played a formal championship, there is little doubt that Allan would have captured the title. He was that good.

Golf was traditionally a game for the wealthy, and the early professionals were considered to be artisans, or the working class. As a result, they had their own club, the St. Andrews Golf Club, which was founded in 1843. Allan was the first prominent member and captain in 1853 and '54.

Despite the distinct cultural differences between artisans and gentry, Allan, Old Tom and other professionals frequently partnered members of the R & A and other clubs in golf matches. The amateurs had great respect for these men as golfers, but would never socialize with them. There was so much admiration for Allan, though, that when he died, R & A members took up a collection to provide an annuity for his widow. His grave in the town cemetery was marked with a substantial tombstone, and his portrait was hung in the Big Room of the R & A clubhouse.

Robertson's club box, or locker, is on display at the St. Andrews Golf Club, where he was an early member and captain.

BOBBY JONES' MARCH ON ST. ANDREWS
by Sidney L. Matthew

No one has studied the life and accomplishments of Bobby Jones more than lawyer Sidney Matthew of Tallahassee, Florida. His two books, The History of Bobby Jones' Golf Clubs *and* Life and Times of Bobby Jones, *explore the details of Jones' life.*

Bobby Jones and St. Andrews: what each meant to the other is one of the greatest love stories in the annals of golf.

Later in life, Jones conceded: "I could take out of my life everything except my experiences at St. Andrews and I would still have a rich and full life." The citizens of St. Andrews were no less extravagant in their appraisal of Jones. They adopted him, gave him his nickname "Bobby," conferred citizenship upon him, named the 10th hole after him, eulogized him, and impressed his legend on the minds and hearts of all who cared to pass along the splendid history to others.

How it all happened is well worth recounting since it had such an inauspicious beginning.

1921
OPEN CHAMPIONSHIP

Centuries of golf history had been recorded by the time Bobby Jones first arrived at St. Andrews in 1921 as a young man of 19. Legions of golfing heroes had already earned the respect and admiration of perhaps the most knowledgeable golf citizenry in the world. Old Tom and Young Tom Morris had displayed their legendary skills on the Old Course links and were revered as beloved native sons. It was perhaps with high hopes that Jones traveled across the Atlantic Ocean on his maiden voyage to display his golf prowess on Scottish soil. Jones had acquitted himself with some aplomb at local amateur events in his native Georgia. He had even caused a stir worthy of mention at the 1916 U.S. Amateur in posting the low medal round.

Jones brought much talent and capability to St. Andrews in 1921. His swing mechanics were sound enough to justify the nickname "Boy Wonder" which the media had given him. The townspeople gave the golfing prodigy much respect after his opening round of 78. He was paired with eventual champion Jock Hutchison, a native St. Andrean and naturalized American. Hutchison was clearly the teacher in that round, with Jones in the front row seat. The veteran made a hole-in-one on the 142-yard eighth hole and nearly holed his drive on the next hole of 303 yards for a double-eagle. Hutchison finished with 72, six strokes less than Jones. In the afternoon, Jones played better and led the entire amateur field with an aggregate of 152.

Jones was positioned for low amateur runner-up honors if not for an act which veteran scribe Henry Longhurst noted "would have quickly been forgotten if committed by an ordinary player." Simply stated, Jones quit in mid-round and ended his inaugural pilgrimage in shame and disgust. He had played the outward half in what he deemed a shocking 46. His bad luck continued on the 10th hole (which later would be renamed in his memory) by making 6. At the short, par-3 11th — one of only two par 3s on the course — Jones hit his tee shot into Hill Bunker, which guards the left side of the green. Sand flew out on his second stroke, but unfortunately not the ball. He did the same on his third and fourth strokes, and perhaps the next, before he lost his composure. Reports of what transpired next are inconsistent. Either Jones left the bunker with the ball in his pocket or he picked up on the green before holing out. Even Jones himself later wrote contradictory accounts.

One of the few eyewitnesses to the spectacle was David Anderson, owner of the nearby Kinburn Hotel, who wrote to the editor of the *St. Andrews Citizen* in October 1958: "Sir: I can remember seeing Bobby Jones tear up his card at the 1921 Open. It happened after Bobby had driven off from the 12th tee. Walking up the fairway, Bobby asked the marker for his card, after a short scrutiny, coolly and deliberately tore it to shreds. Only a handful of spectators were present at the time, certainly not more than a dozen, including the players and caddies in the party."

The legendary golf writer Bernard Darwin erroneously reported that following the mishap at the 11th, Jones "teed up his ball and drove it far away into the Eden." As no writer witnessed the event, several inaccurate and conflicting reports were published, based only on hearsay.

Jones' earliest published account was five years later, in 1926, when he wrote that he had taken 46 strokes at the turn. Later, in his autobiography, *Down the Fairway*, he wrote that he turned in 46 and did not hit his ball into the Eden: "I have some sterling regrets in golf. This is the principal regret — that ever I quit in a competition...But I was a youngster, still making my reputation. And I often have wished I could in some way offer a general apology for picking up my ball on the 11th green of the third round, when I had a short putt left for a horrid 6. It means nothing to the world of golf. But it means something to me. Much more now than it did six years ago, when I took 46 for the first nine of the third round, and a 6 at the tenth and was making a 6 at the 11th, and said to myself, 'What's the use?'

"Of course I continued to play, after tearing up my card — that is a figurative term, by the way — and shot a very good 72 in the fourth round which would have put me in a decent position had I kept on in the competition. (Jones was not required to discontinue play after the incident.)

Scottish professional and clubmaker Bernard Sayers chats with Bobby Jones during the American's first visit to St. Andrews for the 1921 Open Championship. The diminutive Sayers played in every Open Championship from 1880 until 1923.

89

But my showing is not to be mentioned prominently in the same tournament where Jock Hutchison made that tremendous finish, and Roger Wethered, the English amateur, by stepping inadvertently on his own ball, lost a stroke and the championship, going into a tie with Jock, who beat him in the playoff."

Jones' withdrawal from the 1921 Open was his only failure to complete a major championship which he entered. Perhaps the incident formed the basis for his resolve never again to breach the highest ethics of sportsmanship. He had already made great strides in "taming his naturally fiery temperament" by curbing a childish proclivity to throw clubs about.

Nevertheless, out of the ashes of Jones' first visit to St. Andrews, would rise the phoenix of a golf legend unequalled through the generations.

1926
WALKER CUP

During the five-year hiatus between his inaugural pilgrimage to St. Andrews and his return in 1926, young Jones did much studying both in the classroom and on the golf course. He earned his bachelor of science degree in 1922 from Georgia Tech and bachelor of arts in 1925 from Harvard. At the same time, he broke into the major championship ranks with victories in the 1923 U.S. Open (Inwood), 1924 U.S. Amateur (Merion) and 1925 U.S. Amateur (Oakmont). He also worked in the real estate business in Florida, where he was fortunate to spend time with Tommy Armour, the "Silver Scot." It was from Armour that he learned

BOBBY JONES AT ST. ANDREWS
1921
Open Championship

1926
Walker Cup

1927
Open Championship - Winner

1930
Amateur Championship - Winner

1936
Informal visit

1958
World Amateur
Team Championship
Freedom of the City

1972
Memorial service

about the subtleties of the British links.

As was his custom, Jones rarely competed in any tournament other than a major championship. His 1926 schedule included three events in the British Isles: the Amateur at Muirfield, the Walker Cup at St. Andrews and the Open at Royal Lytham and St. Anne's — in that order.

As the reigning U.S. Amateur champion, Jones was favored to win the British version at Muirfield. But he lost in the sixth round to Andrew Jamieson of Glasgow. The winner was New Yorker Jess Sweetser, the first American-born golfer to capture the title. From Muirfield, the contingent of top American and British players traveled up the coast to St. Andrews for the Walker Cup.

Jones defeated the masterful Cyril Tolley in singles by a 12 & 11 margin in a 36-hole match. He also teamed

with fellow Georgian Watts Gunn to conquer the duo of Tolley and Jamieson in foursomes play.

The Americans won the Walker Cup by the narrow margin of six matches to five. Jones originally planned to return home after the Walker Cup, but instead went south to England for the Open Championship at Royal Lytham and St. Anne's. His failure to win the Amateur at Muirfield and subsequent fine play in St. Andrews influenced his decision. Jones won the championship, becoming the first amateur to do so since Harold Hilton in 1897.

1927
OPEN CHAMPIONSHIP

Jones' interest in selling real estate waned in late 1926, and he enrolled at Emory Law School. The raw weather in Atlanta and demands of law school prompted him to put his clubs in the closet from about October until March.

In spite of the winter layoff, Jones began the golf season with a victory in the Southern Open Championship at his home course of East Lake. In the U.S. Open at Oakmont, he finished 11th — his worst of his eight appearances in the championship. (His friend Tommy Armour won that one.)

Up until then, Jones had absolutely no plans to go to St. Andrews to defend his British Open title. However, his disgust with his abysmal showing at Oakmont changed his mind. O.B. Keeler, Jones' biographer and publicist, learned of Jones' entry into the Open while on his way to Paris from New York City on a hon-

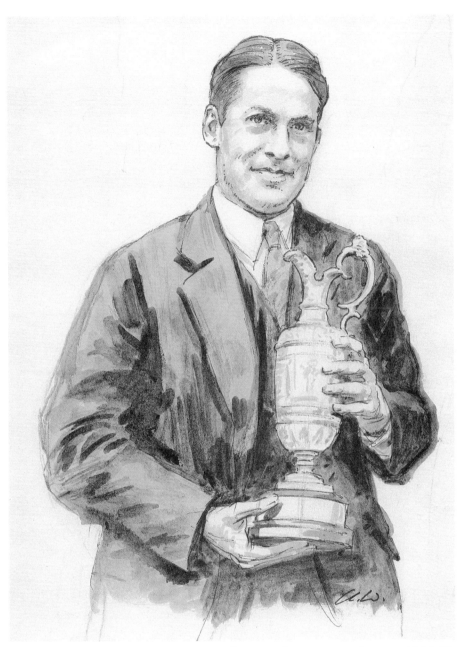

Jones won the second of his three Open Championships at St. Andrews in 1927. He dominated the field, leading after each round and winning by a margin of six strokes.

the second for a bogey — Jones holed a 120-foot putt at the fifth for an eagle 3. He played the first nine holes in 32 and returned in 36, while taking only 29 putts in the round.

Jones led the championship wire-to-wire with succeeding rounds of 72, 73 and 72, for what he termed "the amazing winning aggregate of 285." Never before had such a low score been recorded in the national events of either Britain or America. It was, in effect, a one-man championship with Jones leading the field by six strokes after the first day and by the same margin at the end.

The spectators carried the champion on their shoulders all the way to his hotel, where his father was waiting. "I'm mighty glad that's over," the younger Jones said with a laugh. The Colonel was extremely proud: "I'd rather him win the title here than on any other course in the world and so would Rob."

Jones received yet another great reception from the crowd when he went across to the Royal and Ancient clubhouse for the presentation ceremony outside the main entrance. His acceptance remarks reflected his unusual gift for international diplomacy. He said that winning the championship on the Old Course had been the "ambition of his life." He thanked the crowd for their kindness and stated that he would not take the trophy out of Scotland, but would be pleased to leave it in the custody of the R & A, of which he was proud to be a member. The cheers were deafening.

At the train station, Jones' father emphasized that British sportsmanship was a very real thing and that both

eymoon. Keeler was able to add a side trip to St. Andrews and keep intact his record of being the only man to see Jones win all of his major championships.

Jones arrived in Glasgow on the ship *Transylvania* with only five days to prepare for the championship. His father, Col. Bob Jones, and several friends accompanied him. Although

he lacked confidence in his game, he had no trouble qualifying with a record-tying round of 71 over the New Course.

Whatever uncertainties preceded the 1927 Open were swept away in Jones' spectacular opening round of 68. It was the first time he broke 70 in a major championship. After a wobbly start — requiring a 30-foot putt at he and his son had been overwhelmed by their reception. He spoke of how they deeply appreciated the spectators' traditional sense of admiration for the winner regardless of his nationality. This, despite the fact that his son had come over virtually a stranger and secured their title at a time when Britishers were making great efforts to regain it. This mutual admiration society would be blessed by an increase in membership in the forthcoming great year of 1930.

1930
AMATEUR CHAMPIONSHIP

In the spring of 1930, Bobby Jones had one golfing goal on his mind. He wanted to capture the only championship which had always eluded his grasp: the British Amateur. Jones called it the most important tournament of his life.

Most winters, Jones hung up his clubs. This year, though, he competed in two winter "open" tournaments where he could enjoy heated competition against professionals. In spite of setting the course record twice with rounds of 67-65 in the Savannah Open, Jones still finished behind Horton Smith. He then played what he observed as the "best golf I ever played in any tournament before or since" in posting a 13-stroke victory in the Southeastern Open in Augusta.

The extra preparation paid off for Jones in Britain. His first competition was the Walker Cup at Royal St. George's in Sandwich, where he was playing captain. Jones kept his record flawless by defeating Roger Wethered, the highly regarded Englishman, by a score of 9 & 8 in a 36-hole singles

match. Jones also won his doubles match as the United States denied Britain custody of the cup for the sixth straight time since 1922, when the matches began. He then competed in a one-day, 36-hole event at Sunningdale for the *Golf Illustrated* Gold Vase. Not surprisingly, he won.

Jones could not have been more confident in his game as he journeyed north to St. Andrews for the 41st British Amateur Championship. The format required eight 18-hole rounds of match play, followed by a 36-hole final.

Because of the abundance of short, one-round matches, it was not unusual for a favorite to be eliminated in an early round by a lesser player with a hot putter. This could have been the case in the first round had Jones not played superbly against Syd Roper from Nottinghamshire. Roper showed no fear in the opening holes, posting five 4s in succession for a 1-under-par streak. He even maintained his composure when Jones sank a 140-yard shot from the Cottage Bunker for an eagle 2 on the fourth hole. Roper's brave response was simply to halve Jones with a birdie 4 on the next hole. In spite of his strong play, Roper was 3-down after five holes as Jones opened 3-4-3-2-4.

Roper added only one 5 to 14 consecutive 4s as he finally succumbed to Jones' assault on the course record on the 16th green. (A pair of 4s on the remaining two holes would have tied the course record of 68.) Jones later commented that Roper's steady play would have demolished anyone else in the field.

The next morning, Jones easily dispatched Cowan Shankland 4 & 3 to set up a crowd-pleasing match with Cyril Tolley, the defending champion and two-time titleholder.

Thousands of spectators came for the match. Reporter Bernard Darwin observed that "every man, woman and child in St. Andrews" was on hand to see which titan of golf could master the gale that masqueraded as a "fresh breeze." It blew the sand out of the bunkers while spectators took refuge in the sand hills between shots. Every putt was painted with treachery and emphasized the need to measure not only the quickness of the surface but also the wind's effect.

None of Jones' matches at St. Andrews in 1930 would be decided by more than a couple of strokes. The match with Tolley was no exception. The battle seesawed, and the match came to the 17th all level. The stage was set for a controversy that still remains fodder for lively debate.

At the 17th, Tolley outdrove Jones slightly and was in a better position to avoid the deadly Road Bunker guarding the left of the steeply sloping green. Jones, from the left side of the fairway, was tempted with a daring shot to the flag over the same bunker, but resisted. He knew better.

His best recourse would be to play up the left side of the green, near the 18th tee, past the Road Bunker. He could then play an approach to the flag without hindrance of the notorious bunker. Before making his shot, Jones climbed a hillock and waved at the marshals to move the crowd back from the intended flight line. After he was satisfied that the crowd

On May 31, 1930, Jones accepted the British Amateur trophy from the captain of the R & A, Col. Skene, thus beginning his quest for his unparalleled Grand Slam. Three weeks later, he won the British Open at Royal Liverpool. In July, he won the U.S. Open at Interlachen in Minneapolis. And in September, he captured the U.S. Amateur at Merion in Pennsylvania. Later that year, at the age of 28, he retired from competition.

could move back no further, he hit a 4-iron on line, but a bit too strong. The ball flew into the crowd and was deflected back to the top edge of the green some 40 to 50 feet from the hole.

Some observers, particularly fans of Tolley, asserted that Jones' shot was intentionally played into the crowd. Jones insisted that his efforts to move the spectators back was proof that he never planned a ricochet against the crowd. (Regardless of Jones's intentions, rules officials decided thereafter that no part of a championship gallery should be allowed to the left of the green.)

Tolley pulled his second shot slightly and came to rest to the left of the green with the devilish Road Bunker intervening. It was not the place to be. At this point, a Jones two-putt appeared certain to win the hole. But Tolley pulled off a miracle with a deft pitch over the bunker. Accounts state that the pitch was "bravely judged so that it trembled momentarily on the edge of the bunker before trickling down a foot from the hole." In an unexpected change of events, Tolley appeared to be back in the match with a probable 4 for a halve. Then Jones left his approach putt some 8 feet from the hole. But he was relentless as his slippery putt fell into the hole to move the drama to the 18th, all even.

Jones later acknowledged that Tolley's third shot "has never been surpassed for exquisitely beautiful execution." Tolley himself agreed it was the finest shot of his life.

The 18th was also halved, taking the match back to the first hole with

each player understandably exhausted. Tolley's second shot ended left of the green, and his chip was slightly closer to the hole than his opponent's 10-foot birdie putt. Even though the birdie attempt failed, Jones managed a stymie by obstructing Tolley's line to the hole and emerged the victor.

Jones retired George O. Watt of Monifieth in his fourth-round match by a margin of 5 & 4. In each of the following two matches, against American Jimmy Johnston and Scot Eric Fiddian, Jones was at one point 4-up. Even so, he needed to make an 8-foot putt at the home hole to turn back Johnston's late charge, and he needed a sub-par round to turn back Fiddian.

The semifinal match against fellow Walker Cupper George Voigt, from New York, was a different story. Jones broke with his tradition of waiting until all competition was completed before consuming an alcoholic beverage. Before the afternoon match Jones had a glass of sherry to calm his nerves. Mixed with his natural adrenaline, the wine's effect was multiplied. It wasn't until the match was in the latter holes before Jones could properly focus his blurred vision. By that time, Voigt had accumulated a seemingly convincing 2-up advantage with only five holes remaining to play. But on the 14th hole, Voigt fortuitously drove out of bounds, providing Jones the opening he needed. An onslaught of Jones' best golf thereafter gobbled up Voigt's lead until Jones secured victory on the home hole where Voigt tragically three-putted. (In the 13 matches Jones played that year in winning the British and U.S. Amateur titles, Voight was

the only player to have Jones more than 1-down.)

Jones' 36-hole final match was played on Saturday against Roger Wethered, the 1923 Amateur Champion and runner-up in the 1921 Open at the Old Course.

Enormous crowds gathered for the closing contest: about 6,000 persons in the morning and almost 15,000 in the afternoon. "Motor cars streamed into the city from all quarters," the local newspaper reported. "Thousands arrived by rail, and the various buses were packed."

The match began with rather ordinary play and, although Jones was 1-up by the 10th hole, he was concerned with his putting accuracy. By the end of the morning round, his medal score of 71 gave him a 4-up advantage. But he admitted that he was far from comfortable.

Jones had what he termed a "touch-and-go" start in the afternoon. He was out in 37, Wethered in 38. The match concluded at the 12th with the margin at 7 & 6. Jones was 2-under 4s.

Wethered at once congratulated Jones on his deserved victory. Then the surging crowd of cheering admirers surrounded Jones. The stewards and policemen struggled in the difficult task of escorting the champion on a half-hour journey from the links to his quarters at the Grand Hotel.

The champion, face drawn and haggard from the week's ordeal of matches, described his state: "I don't think I was ever so happy about any golf event in my life… I was not confident with my putts today, but then Roger was missing them, and I began to feel that the difficult greens must

When Jones showed up in St. Andrews for a casual round in 1936, word of his arrival spread like wildfire. As usual, he accommodated his adoring fans by signing autographs.

have something to do with it...I've been lucky but I'm glad. I shall do my best at Hoylake [in the upcoming Open Championship] but I shall not worry if I do not win there. This was the big thing for me."

The victor changed into a smart gray suit and made his way through the sea of spectators to the steps of the R & A clubhouse to accept the championship cup. The speeches were amplified by microphone and could be heard well beyond Granny Clark's Wynd (the road crossing the links) and from the windows of houses and

hotels nearby. The first and 18th fairways were blanketed with thousands of exuberant spectators.

Col. P.G.M. Skene, captain of the R & A, remarked about the keenness of the play, especially the magnificent fight between Jones and Tolley. He then asked the champion to come and accept the trophy while stating that although the champion was from the other side of the Atlantic, they in St. Andrews could "claim a bit of him as he was a member of the Royal and Ancient Club."

After several minutes of thunderous applause and cheering, Jones observed: "I must say how happy I am to have won this cup. I have never worked harder or suffered more than in trying to get it. It has been said that I enjoyed the Tolley match, but, much as I love Cyril, I would not have been glad to see him in the next round. (Laughter.) I have said before that St. Andrews has been a little bit too good to me when I was lucky enough to win the Open here, but I want to say now that it has made me feel happier than the winning of any other cup in the past."

Jones left St. Andrews for Paris, where he vacationed with his wife for a week. Then he went to England, where he won the Open Championship with a record-breaking score at Hoylake. Following a ticker-tape parade in New York, Jones finished out the season with victories in the U.S. Open and U.S. Amateur. Having achieved his lofty goal — later named the Grand Slam — the 28-year-old Jones retired from competition.

95

1936
INFORMAL VISIT

In 1936, the Olympic Games were held in Berlin and Jones' friend from Georgia, hurdler Forrest "Spec" Towns, was favored to win a gold medal. Jones and a few friends agreed that the event would serve as a "splendid excuse for playing golf in Britain," and the trip was soon arranged.

The contingent arrived in London, played Sunningdale and then headed north to Gleneagles in Scotland. Jones then decided a pilgrimage to St. Andrews was in order. "I could not leave here without playing at St. Andrews," he said.

A chauffeur was dispatched to St. Andrews to place four names in the ballot for a tee time at the Old Course: F. Hodgson, D. Garlington, E. Kelley, and R.T. Jones Jr.

The party traveled to St. Andrews in the morning and had lunch at the R & A clubhouse. Looking out a window, they noticed several thousand townspeople assembled down the length of the first fairway. Jones concluded that he had the misfortune of attempting to play a private match during an important championship. Little did he know that the news of his coming had spread rapidly throughout the town. Businesses closed their doors as the locals eagerly awaited their hero.

The scheduled match was spontaneously revised and after a few holes, only Jones and Willie Auchterlonie, the R & A's honorary professional, continued to play. The gallery had swelled to 4,000.

Jones rose to the occasion. He later described the day as the "best golf I had played for four years and certainly never since." At the sixth he was faced with a choice of the old St. Andrews run-up shot or a fancy pitch. Jones said to himself, "Look, Jones, these people are all expecting you to play that run-up, so don't you funk it." The ball rolled up to the green and finished six feet from the flag. Jones holed it for a 3. Inspired by the "home-town crowd," Jones made 2 at the par-3 eighth and turned in 32. Perhaps it was poetic justice that Jones and "Old Man Par" each acquitted themselves with dignity on that day as

Jones was round in 71 or 72 — depending on which account you read.

Jones later spoke of the event: "I shall never forget that round. It was not anything like a serious golf match, but it was a wonderful experience. There was sort of a holiday mood in the crowd. It seemed, or they made it appear at least, that they were just glad to see me back, and however I played golf was all right with them, only they wanted to see it."

1958
WORLD AMATEUR
TEAM CHAMPIONSHIP
AND
FREEMASON CEREMONY

Bobby Jones dreamed of a return to Britain after 1936, but never gave it serious consideration until the inaugural World Team Amateur Championship was scheduled for St. Andrews. Jones accepted the duty of captain for the American team and for the first time traveled by airplane across the Atlantic. By this time his affliction with syringeomyelia, a debilitating neurological disease, had long ended his days as a golfer.

Walking with the aid of two canes toward Rusack's Hotel, Jones commented, "It's been a long time getting back — 22 years. But it's worth waiting for." With the Scottish twilight shining on the links, Jones quipped, "I'm going to get in my electric buggy and travel all over the Old Course. It will be the first buggy ever to go round there and I bet you it'll be the last." Jones' words were never so accurate, as no buggies (motorized golf carts) are permitted to this day on the Old Course.

In this contest, the Americans fought a hard battle, but the Australian team prevailed to win the Eisenhower Cup.

But it was not on the links where Jones would shine on this trip. The Younger Graduation Hall of St. Andrews University on the evening of October 9, 1958, was the venue for what Jones called the "most impressive and emotional experience" in his life.

The town clerk had cabled Jones a month before inquiring if he would accept the honor of being a "Freeman of St. Andrews." Jones accepted, but did not really consider the matter to be more significant than receiving the perfunctory key to the city, of which he already had a key ring full.

Upon arriving at St. Andrews, Jones was given a short history of the honor, including the fact that he would be the second American — Benjamin Franklin being the first in 1759 — to receive such an honor. The benefits were tantamount to nothing less than citizenship with the traditional rights to hunt rabbits, dig divots, and even bleach his laundry on the first and 18th fairways near the Swilken Burn.

Jones met the town clerk's request for an advance copy of his speech with a nervous reply that he was still working on it. Jones did prepare essential notes, but he would trust his natural instincts of carefully weighing the circumstances and measuring his reply on the spot ex tempore.

Seventeen-hundred people filled Younger Hall to capacity on the appointed evening. Some of those waiting outside would write letters to the editor of the *St. Andrews Citizen*

In 1958, Jones became the seventh individual in the history of St. Andrews to be granted the Freedom of the City by the Town Council. Other recipients of the prestigious honor include Benjamin Franklin and Edward, Duke of Windsor. In his heartfelt acceptance speech, Jones reminisced about his visits to St. Andrews and proclaimed "that this is the finest thing that has ever happened to me."

complaining that another thousand people should have been anticipated for this singular historical event.

The town clerk, adorned in white wig and crimson robe, opened the ceremony with a prayer and reading of the citation. Then, Provost Robert Leonard, resplendent in an ermine-trimmed robe adorned with the chains of office, rose to speak about St. Andrews' newest citizen. The short history of Jones' initial misunderstanding and dislike of the Old Course in 1921 was embellished by the subsequent spawning of a love affair unequaled in give and take between the champion and the people. Leonard remarked, "As representative of St. Andrews, we wish to honor Mr. Jones because we feel drawn to him by ties of affection and personal regard of a

particular cordial nature, and because we know that he himself has declared his own enduring affection for the place and for its people."

Jones was then invited to sign the Burgess Roll, followed by presentation of a beautifully engraved silver casket with the scroll conferring the Freedom honor. Jones whispered that he did not desire any assistance in rising from his chair and awkwardly shuffled to the podium. He positioned himself and began to weave a theme of friendship and admiration that, at times, compelled him to pause lest he be so overcome with emotion that he couldn't continue. "I just want to say to you that this is the finest thing that has ever happened to me." Jones reminisced about his impetuous withdrawal from the 1921 Open at

the "ripe old age of 19 years" and admitted that he didn't know much about golf then. However, after talking to a lot of transplanted Scots and much studying, Jones admitted he never lost another contest on the Old Course. He recalled the miniature British Amateur trophy sent following the Grand Slam and treasured his visit in 1936 when the townspeople locked their stores and walked the fairways while witnessing the best golf he had played in years.

Jones concluded his speech with the memorable observation, "I could take out of my life everything except my experiences at St. Andrews and I would still have a rich and full life." At the end of his remarks, the audience stood and regaled him with "For He's a Jolly Good Fellow" and "Will Ye No' Come Back Again?". Jones then amazed everyone by walking unassisted to his electric cart and leaving the hall. Henry Longhurst observed that it was several minutes before anyone could speak in a calm voice.

THE END

On December 18, 1971, golfers on the Old Course stopped their play as the flag on the R & A clubhouse was lowered to half-staff. News had been received that Bobby Jones had died.

A memorial service was held in St. Andrews on May 4, 1972, at the Holy Trinity Church. A touching tribute was delivered by Roger Wethered, who first competed against Jones 50 years earlier in the 1922 Walker Cup. Following the service, there was a procession of dignitaries through the streets, led by a hall porter carrying one of the R & A's ceremonial silver clubs.

"BUB"

by Robert Tyre Jones IV

Bobby Jones was formally known as Robert Tyre Jones Jr. He was named after his grandfather. Bobby and his wife, Mary, had two daughters and a son. Their son, Robert Tyre Jones III, also had a son, Atlantan Robert Tyre Jones IV, who wrote the following recollection. Bob was 14 years old when his grandfather died in 1971.

Most of the stories that I know about St. Andrews I learned from my father. This was because my grandfather would not talk about golf with me. "Bub" (my family's nickname for my grandfather) felt that there were many topics which we could discuss and did not want golf to be one of them. He believed that the pressure of carrying the "Bob Jones" name and the expectations that people would have of my golf game might be very difficult to overcome. So we would talk about all sorts of things but never would we talk about golf. (However, by the time he told me this I was already hooked on the game.)

I was introduced to St. Andrews as a young child when I noticed the Alister Mackenzie line drawing of the Old Course which hung in our den. My father called it the greatest golf course in the world and said that Bub had learned more about golf and about himself on that course than on any other. I would look at that plan of the course and wonder what it was about that place that was so special.

As I was older, I began to hear the stories about Bub and St. Andrews and I began to learn more about the importance of the place in the life of my family.

Before my first golf tournament at our home club, my parents told me about Bub's first Open on the Old Course. Fixing me in place with firm parental stares, they told about how Bub picked up his ball on the 11th hole and disqualified himself from the championship. They emphasized that was the only time in his career that he withdrew from a championship and it was something that he regretted deeply. "Bub," my father said, "always believed that there was a lot which you could learn about golf and about yourself when things were not going well."

The Jones presence at St. Andrews has always been greeted with a certain amount of festivity. This was certainly the case when Bub returned to St. Andrews in 1936 and the whole town came out to witness a casual round of golf. My father had a slightly different experience.

In the 1950s, my father visited Scotland and had the good fortune of playing his first round on the Old Course. Dad was a good player in his own right, winning a number of regional championships and playing several times in the U.S. Amateur. When he arrived at the first tee of the Old Course, he was startled to find what looked like several hundred people waiting for him. Dad discovered that they had all shown up to watch "Bobby's son" play the Old Course.

"I've never been as nervous as I was at that moment," Dad told me. "I stood on the first tee and my knees were shaking. I hit a very solid 3-wood down by the Swilken Burn. It was a fantastic shot. But the crowd silently watched the shot and then silently walked down the fairway.

"Well, when I got to the ball, I took out a sand wedge. I had a simple flip wedge of about 40 yards to the pin. I settled down over the ball, and proceeded to cold shank it into the water. And when I looked up, all of the townspeople were heading back in." Dad explained that "St. Andrews galleries expect excellence, but they will also not gawk at a painful death."

Around the Jones house, the most vividly recalled and frequently recounted story was when Bub received the Freedom of the Burgh in 1958. When I was a child, I used to be fascinated by a sterling silver box, called a casket, that sat on a small table in my grandparents' living room. My grandmother — who we called "Neenah" — pronounced it "cahskat" to distinguish it from a receptacle for burial.

Bub considered this Freedom the greatest honor that he was ever awarded. When I was 12, my father sat me down in front of the casket. He lifted the hinged lid, removed the elaborate scroll and had me read it aloud in what seemed to me, on later reflection, to be some sort of familial rite of passage. My father then looked me straight in the eye and quoted from memory the remarks about friendship which Bub made at the presentation ceremony.

The words came from one of my grandfather's books:

> "Friends are a man's priceless treasures, and a life rich in friendship is full indeed. When I say, with due regard for the meaning of the word, that I am your friend, I have pledged to you the ultimate in loyalty and devotion. In some respects friendship may even transcend love, for in true friendship there is no place for jealousy. When, without more, I say that you are my friends, it is possible that I am imposing upon you a greater burden than you are willing to assume. But when you have made me aware on many occasions that you have a kindly feeling toward me, and when you have honored me by every means at your command, then when I call you friend, I am at once affirming my high regard and affection for you and declaring my complete faith in you and trust in the sincerity of your expressions."

My father and I sat in silence for a moment. "Son," my dad finally said, "The most important thing in the world is friendship. That's an important lesson and you need to learn it as early in life as you can."

To this day, when I hear the words "St. Andrews," I always think of friendship.

"I have already said hundreds of times that I like it better than any golf course I have ever played and although I have played it many, many times, its charm for me increases with every round."

— Bobby Jones

99

SIX TRIES ON THE OLD COURSE

by Arnold Palmer

Palmer's initial visit to St. Andrews for the 1960 Open was instrumental in renewing worldwide interest in the oldest of golf championships. Although Arnie captured the title in 1961 and repeated in '62, he never won over the Old Course.

Golf has been part of my life for as long as I can remember. I can scarcely recall when that did not include St. Andrews, even while I was growing up in Latrobe, a small town in Western Pennsylvania — over 3,000 miles from Scotland. My father, Deacon, was a golf professional, and "Pap," as we called him, told me about the origins of golf as I learned to play the game.

What a grand place that must be, St. Andrews, we thought. This was just after the Great Depression, and the chances then that either Deacon or Arnold Palmer would ever see Scotland with his own eyes was remote, at best.

Some people will remember my year of 1960 for winning the U.S. Open, or the second of my four Masters titles, but I am also particularly fond of 1960 because that was the year I took Pap to St. Andrews — for my first British Open Championship.

I finished in second place, suffering one of the biggest disappointments of my entire career, but we were having the times of our lives that week, just to be in St. Andrews. The old grey town was more wonderful than we could ever have imagined, as we saw the history and traditions of the game at every turn... Tom Morris' shop... Grannie Clark's Wynd... arriving for the first time at the second tee in a practice round and wondering "Where's the fairway?"... the Scottish bunkers, each with stories to tell and its own name, such as the Principal's Nose... the Road Hole, oh, the dreaded Road Hole, as I would soon discover... and the Valley of Sin.

Memories of St. Andrews and the Open Championship — including 1960, 1970, 1978, 1984 and 1990 — are inseparable for me. I have never known the "other" St. Andrews, never looked from my hotel window at Rusack's Marine without seeing the huge spectator stands at the 18th green and the tented village in the distance. Never have I had the opportunity to take a quiet dinner in the town or to walk along the beach without another person in sight.

I would like to know St. Andrews from that other perspective. Few people may know this, but I am a member of both the Royal and Ancient Golf Club and the New Golf Club. It would be a tremendous thrill to play in the R & A's Autumn Medal, then later go over to the New Club for a friendly drink with the other members. When it comes to enjoying golf as a social game, I am like anyone else.

Nearly all my experiences in St. Andrews have been centered on the Open Championship. Sadly, the memories are laced with disappointment. But I have a sense of pride, as well, and there are many fond memories of the warmth of the Scottish people, who supported me as if I were one of their own, and then there's the great relationship with my caddie of over 30 years, Tip Anderson.

The Open Championship is one of the world's premier golf events, perhaps the most important title in the game, depending on how you rate golf's four major events. People have credited me with having had something to do with the present status of the Open Championship and, if that is true, I am honored to have had a role in restoring golf's oldest championship to the position that it deserves.

In the years before I first came to St. Andrews, I had watched what had happened to the Open Championship and regretted that, because of the indifference of the leading American players at that time, the Open had become very much a British Commonwealth event. On the other hand, I felt that the Open was one of golf's really great championships and ought to be recognized as such.

Without taking anything at all from Kel Nagle, who beat me by one stroke in 1960, I really did think I was going to win, and I felt — and still feel — that I should have won. But I didn't win, and I guess that's just how golf is. Mostly, the fault was in my putting or my inability to read the greens. Tip Anderson may have misread a few, too. We kept seeing breaks — or "borrows," as the Scots called them — that did not exist. And there was the 17th, a hole which I dislike to this day. Mind you, I love the Old Course, but I have never come to terms with the Road Hole, as the 17th has always been known. I keep trying to play it as a par 4 on the card, rather than a par 5, which is more the way it plays.

Despite the Road Hole, I have always believed that I would have won the 1960 Open, if not for the rain that forced a postponement of the final round until Saturday, rather than having two rounds Friday, as was the schedule in those days. I did play well Saturday, my score was 68, but not as well as I would have done against the field, had we played on through Friday afternoon.

I felt so strongly that would be my date with destiny, that I would have worn out the others. I was fired up, and I just knew I would play that much better than they would.

Not winning the Open Championship in St. Andrews made me all the more determined to return and win, which I did in 1961 at Royal Birkdale and in 1962 at Troon. When I did not play at St. Andrews in 1964, I lent my putter and my caddie, Tip Anderson, to Tony Lema, who went on to win. But I never forgot the disappointment of not winning that first Open at St. Andrews. How proud Pap and I would have been to go home with that old claret jug, the British Open trophy, under our airline seats.

It must have been fate. Just as in what I thought would be my final Open in 1990 at St. Andrews, everyone knew that my rounds of 73 and 71 would be more than enough to assure a place for the final 36 holes. Once again, I had a stroke too many. I had so looked forward to walking up the 18th fairway that Sunday afternoon, but I had many good years of the Open. I enjoyed the courses, enjoyed the people, and made a lot of friends. I had seen the Open Championship grow from St. Andrews of 1960.

Now, I've been invited back for another chance in 1995. But when I go back to St. Andrews again in the future, I'll be just another member of the Royal and Ancient, or the New Club, there for the same reason as everyone else — because it is St. Andrews, and there couldn't be a more perfect place for golf on earth.

"It would be a tremendous thrill to play in the R & A's Autumn Medal, then go over to the New Club for a friendly drink with the other members."

TIP ANDERSON

On Arnold Palmer's first visit to Great Britain in 1960, he linked up with caddie Tip Anderson and finished second in the Open at St. Andrews. Anderson was two years younger than the 30-year-old superstar, and the two made a formidable team. The following year at Royal Birkdale they reunited to win the Open and then repeated at Troon in 1962. Since that time Palmer has relied exclusively on Anderson to guide him in the Open, Ryder Cup and other championships in the British Isles.

The duo's most recent stint in the limelight was in the 1994 British Senior Open, where the 64-year-old Palmer tied for the first-round lead. He finished the championship in fourth place.

The relationship has served both men well. Palmer's record speaks for itself. Anderson, a career caddie, has become a celebrity, too; he is by far the most requested caddie in St. Andrews. Anderson summed up his qualifications in a 1990 *New York Times* article: "Forgive my lack of modesty, but I am the most experienced and best regular caddie at the Old Course at St. Andrews. I have caddied there at least four times a week for the last 44 years, since I was 14 years old."

Tip Anderson Jr. has caddied for Arnold Palmer in 28 British Opens, starting with the 1960 Championship.

Alastair Johnston, born in Glasgow and educated at the University of Strathclyde, manages business affairs for Arnold Palmer. He now resides in Cleveland, Ohio, where he is senior executive vice-president for International Management Group (IMG), the organization founded by Palmer's original manager, Mark McCormack. Johnston has written several books on early golf history.

Tip Anderson's father, Tip Sr. (inset), and grandfather, both caddies in St. Andrews, lived in this house on South Street.

The 1995 Open Championship will be Nicklaus' fifth at St. Andrews.

MY FAVORITE PLACE

by Jack Nicklaus

Jack Nicklaus, winner of back-to-back Open Championships at St. Andrews in 1970 and 1978, is only the fourth player to win two Opens over the Old Course and the first since James Braid in 1905 and 1910.

Nicklaus receives the Open Championship trophy in 1970 from Willie Whitelaw, captain of the Royal and Ancient Golf Club.

I first came to Scotland in 1959 to play in the Walker Cup matches, and I still cringe at the thought of the raw, crewcut, overconfident 19-year-old who was sure he could take apart both the Muirfield course and everyone on it without batting an eye. My love for this country began on that first trip, and it has grown stronger and deeper with each succeeding visit. I hope the passage of time has at least partly made up for a certain brashness during my first visit.

I love the style and the atmosphere of Scottish golf, and the great Scottish linksland courses. I am also in constant awe of the variety and beauty of the

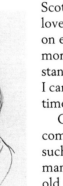

Scottish terrain. But what has always made me love Scotland the most is the people. Nowhere on earth have I been received more warmly, more affectionately, or with greater understanding than by the people of this country. I can assure you that the memories of my times here will never fade.

Of all my memories, the richest have come from St. Andrews, this lovely city of such great lore and legend, renowned for so many qualities and achievements beyond the old and noble game. One thing I have learned is that there always have been, and always will be, conflicting opinions on the Old Course, where every few years the world's finest players compete for the most cherished international golf championship on earth.

Be that as it may, it is unimaginable to me how any true golfer — anyone who really cares about the game — can fail to enjoy and appreciate St. Andrews.

I came to St. Andrews the first time more than 30 years ago to play in the Open Championship of 1964, and I came back to win in 1970 and again in 1978. It was on that third visit that I had one of the most memorable experiences of my golfing life. On that last day, walking down the 18th fairway to my third Open Championship victory was a moment I will cherish forever. It is times such as that one which make me certain that there is only one home of golf: St. Andrews. This is where the greatest game of all truly began, and where its history and tradition will remain for centuries to come. As I have said many times before, this is my favorite place in all the golfing world.

The 1995 Open will be the 34th consecutive one in which I've played. Winning three of them — two at St. Andrews — is very special to me. My hope now is to return to St. Andrews and to have one of my sons compete alongside me for the historic title.

105

St. Andreans have great respect for Jack Nicklaus. He's an honorary member of both the St. Andrews and the Royal and Ancient golf clubs and has an honorary degree from the University of St. Andrews.

Jack Nicklaus tees off on the final hole of an 18-hole playoff with Doug Sanders for the 1970 Open Championship. Had Sanders holed a short putt on the 72nd hole of regulation play, he would have been champion. This Nicklaus drive rolled over the green and set up an 8-foot birdie putt to squelch a late charge from Sanders by a single stroke.

THE PLACE WITH THE MAGIC

by Nick Faldo

1990

108

Nick Faldo began making headlines in 1975 as a teenager, when he won both the English Amateur and British Youth's titles. Since then he has established himself as one of the top British golfers of the modern era. Faldo has won five majors: the 1987, '90 and '92 Opens, and back-to-back Masters in 1989 and '90. In team competition, he has represented Europe in nine Ryder Cups and England twice in the World Cup and seven times in the Dunhill Cup at St. Andrews.

What does St. Andrews mean to me? Let me put it this way: Whichever sport you play you want to win in the right place. I always wanted to win the Open — maybe several Opens — and above all, I wanted to win the Open at St. Andrews.

Although I won my first Open at Muirfield, the Old Course is the place with the magic. It has the town wrapped all around it, with all the history. It's a magical place. You can sense that. Gill, my wife, has never played golf in her life, yet when she goes there she says, "I know what you mean now." We have gone to see the cathedral, all the tombstones and that sort of thing. These are the things that make St. Andrews quite something.

I am pleased that I played so well when I won on the Old Course in 1990. I missed only three greens and one of those, the 17th, was a deliberate miss. I played a lot of good iron shots, I drove the ball well. Although the fairways are big, you still need to go down the correct side. Block the odd shot and you start worrying about how you're going to get out without taking too many risks. I was in one bunker all week — it was on the fourth on the last day.

It is very easy at St. Andrews to be fractionally off line and then end up 30 yards from the hole. You only have to hit the ball slightly off center, and it takes the wrong bump and goes a bit long. And putting from 30 yards can be hard work. Luckily, I managed to be closer than that; in fact, I don't think I was ever more than 30 feet from the hole all week. Then, it seems to me as I look back, that every time I had a makeable putt, I holed it.

I have played three Opens at St. Andrews: in 1978, 1984 and 1990. I even shared the course record after shooting a 65 in the 1979 PGA. I also have played in the Dunhill Cup there. The course record didn't last long. They're shooting 62s now. On a calm, damp day you can do that. Maybe a 60 is next, who knows?

The longest putt I have holed in my life was on the Old Course during the 1979 PGA. It was from the front-left edge of the fourth green and it was paced off at 34 yards. That putt was just slightly longer than the amazing one I made at Augusta a few years ago.

You will never have four calm days at St. Andrews. Even at the height of summer there is always a breeze. It is a great golf course with championship pins, and we're lucky because we only play the course when it has championship pins.

St. Andrews has some great holes. The 14th is one of the best par 5s in the world. The 11th, over that bunker, is wicked. You've only got three yards with which to work. The 17th is always very tough. Whether you like it or not, it's a brute of a hole. Actually, I think it's a good, but not great, hole. If you hit it straight down the middle of the fairway and they've put the pin behind the Road Hole Bunker, then you don't have a shot.

Over the years I have decided to go left of that green. I think that's a far better percentage shot because then you are chipping back up the green and looking at a good chance of making four. If you go to the right, you can either end up short and you won't make four from there, or you can go over the green and you won't make four from there. It is definitely the percentage shot to go left.

I was lucky because I was given a wonderful guide to St. Andrews by Gerald Micklem before I played it for the first time. It consisted of notes he had written specially for me in his rather squiggly writing. They were on foolscap paper, and my father had to decode them and put them on index cards. I took them with me and read them as I played the course the first few times.

They said things like the best line to hit from each tee. Down the first go left, down the second and the third go right, more right than people would have you believe. Gerald was quoted once as saying, "if something goes wrong as surely it will, you mustn't get cross at St. Andrews. The Old Course must be treated sympathetically. Don't try and fight it. Try to understand it. This applies to St. Andrews more than perhaps 99 percent of the courses I know in the world." I don't think it is true any more. St. Andrews is one of the easier courses we play, unless the weather is a howling gale.

Gill and I have tried to find those notes because we would like to give them to the golf museum there. We've turned the house upside down, but I think we must have lost them in one of our moves. A shame.

I shall remember my victory at St. Andrews in 1990 forever. By the time I am old and gray it will have sunk in a little more — that my name is next to all the great names that have played golf since the game started. That is a really nice feeling, and that is what winning at St. Andrews means to me.

Faldo hits an approach shot to the 18th green in the 1990 Open Championship as his Swedish caddie, Fanny Sunesson, looks on. The steward in the foreground is signaling "quiet" to the gallery.

BRITISH OPEN CHAMPIONS AT ST. ANDREWS

1873	TOM KIDD
1876	BOB MARTIN
1879	JAMIE ANDERSON
1882	BOB FERGUSON
1885	BOB MARTIN
1888	JACK BURNS
1891	HUGH KIRKALDY
1895	J.H. TAYLOR
1900	J.H. TAYLOR
1905	JAMES BRAID
1910	JAMES BRAID
1921	JOCK HUTCHISON
1927	ROBERT T. JONES JR.
1933	DENNY SHUTE
1939	RICHARD BURTON
1946	SAM SNEAD
1955	PETER THOMSON
1957	BOBBY LOCKE
1960	KEL NAGLE
1964	TONY LEMA
1970	JACK NICKLAUS
1978	JACK NICKLAUS
1984	SEVE BALLESTEROS
1990	NICK FALDO

Nick Faldo celebrates after two-putting the final green for a five-stroke margin of victory in the 1990 Open. His 18-under-par 270 set a new record for the championship. At the presentation ceremony the Red Arrows, the Royal Air Force aerobatic team, did a low-level flyby in recognition of the Englishman's second Open win.

1984

Since the mid-1970s, Seve Ballesteros has been winning golf championships throughout the world. In addition to winning three Open Championships, two Masters and playing on seven Ryder Cup teams, the Spaniard has won dozens of tournaments in the United States, United Kingdom, Europe and the Far East.

FOND MEMORIES

by Severiano Ballesteros

The first time I ever visited the golf courses at St. Andrews, my mind drifted back to my childhood days, when I was about 7 or 8 years old and was just learning to play golf. It was at a place close to our family home in Pedrena, Spain — at a small beach very near the local golf course.

To tell the truth, the scene of that beach in Pedrena, which nowadays is a driving range, was so similar to what I saw in St. Andrews that I felt myself carried back to my early boyhood days, as if through a time tunnel. Since then I have always felt some special preference for St. Andrews, first because it reminded me of my childhood, and second, because I had the honor of winning the Open there in 1984.

I will never forget the mental image of the 18th hole when I sank my last putt to win the most prestigious tournament in the world. Anybody can speak wonders about St. Andrews, but few can express such high emotions as a golfer when he wins the biggest tournament on the planet in golf's most ancient arena.

Whenever the Open returns to St. Andrews, I hope to be present in order to feel the same thrill as before. But most of all, I look forward to sharing the excitement of the Old Course with the Scottish golf fans, to whom I owe so much gratitude for their support whenever I play in their wonderful country.

◆

Seve's fist-pumping victory celebration at the '84 Open ranks as one of championship golf's most emotional moments.

◆

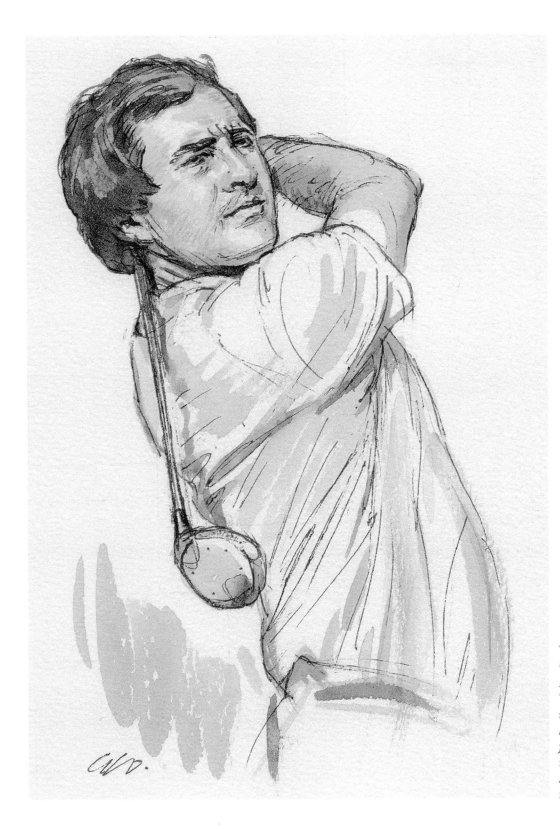

113

The finish of the 1984 Open was a duel between Ballesteros and Tom Watson. The Spaniard emerged as the victor by two strokes when he holed a birdie putt on the final hole while the American was having problems with the stone wall along the road by the 17th green.

1960

Australian Kel Nagle has an international reputation. He won national open championships in Great Britain, France, Australia, New Zealand and Canada. He also tied for first in the 1965 U.S. Open, but lost to Gary Player in a playoff.

TOUGH COMPETITION

by Kel Nagle

I had read so much about the Old Course of St. Andrews before I arrived in 1960 that I really did not know what to expect. My first impression was that it was very unusual — two fairways wide with mostly large and rolling double greens. On a calm day you think to yourself, "What an easy golf course." But when the tide changes and the wind blows, the "old lady," as she is called, really shows her teeth.

When you walk out onto the first tee and look down to the Swilken Burn in front of the green, the feeling that comes over you is unbelievable. My favorite view is from the 14th tee looking back across the Beardies (a group of deep bunkers) to the clubhouse and the town with its dark gray buildings.

I especially enjoyed walking around and looking at the town, the churches and the ruins by the sea. During the championship, I was fortunate enough to stay in Forgan's house, right beside the 18th green. There I witnessed all the comings and goings of people walking their dogs or going over to the Eden Course with clubs in hand. They have such lovely, long evenings in Scotland that you can play golf up to 11 o'clock at night.

Most of all, I enjoyed watching clubmaker Laurie Auchterlonie work on his favorite wooden putters. He was a real craftsman. Although he sold them for five pounds, they were worth five times that amount, considering all the time he spent working on them. His library of golf books also was something to see.

The R & A clubhouse, with its trophy room vault containing the championship belt and silver clubs, was a sight to see. A trip to the Royal and Ancient, if at all possible, is an experience you will never regret. Just to walk on the hallowed grounds is a treat — with the beautiful turf and the greens that are so true. I think Scottish turf is the best in the world as the ball sits nicely so you can take a nice crisp divot.

I get so emotional about the town that I nearly forgot to write about winning the Open Championship. Peter Thomson and I did a bit of globetrotting on our way to St. Andrews. First, we took a little trip to the States and played in the Colonial Invitation at Fort Worth, Texas. This is where I assembled a new set of clubs; I found a MacGregor driver and borrowed a set of Spalding irons. Like magic, I could place a drive anywhere I wanted, and the irons were perfect. I finished second in the tournament.

We then went to Portmarnock in Ireland for the World Cup Team Championship. As defending champions, Peter and I played well enough to finish third. Then it was on to Scotland for the Open Championship. Peter — who had won the Open in 1955, the last time it was played in St. Andrews — was impressed with my game. He said, "I think you can win the Open. I'll take you around and show you where to go."

We practiced for three days together before having to qualify over 36 holes. (Everyone played a total of six rounds in those days.) The Open started, and Roberto DeVicenzo led the first two rounds with 67-67, and I was next with 69-67. After me was Arnold Palmer, who was five shots back. (Palmer had already won the Masters and U.S. Open that year and was going for the Grand Slam.) Roberto and I were paired together for the final 36 holes, which were all played on Friday in those days. I had 71 in the third round and Roberto had a 75. We had just finished putting out on the last green when the heavens opened with such a deluge of rain the course was unplayable. The bunkers were full and the Valley of Sin in front of the 18th green was like a lake, so the Championship Committee rescheduled the fourth round for Saturday.

There was not a lot of drama in the last round until the last few holes, when Arnie began making a charge in the group just ahead of Roberto and me. At this point, Palmer was only two shots behind me. He then made a great 4 from the road on 17. (I must mention that I was lucky enough to make 3 on that tricky hole by sinking a 40-foot putt from the road in the first round!) Anyway, Arnie was on the final hole while I was on the 17th in two, a long way from the flag. I putted to about 8 feet, and by this time Arnold had a 6-or 8-foot birdie putt on the last green. I decided to wait and see what happened, and when the roar went up, I knew he had made birdie. So now my 8-foot putt was very crucial. It looked in all the way, just the right speed with a right-to-left borrow. I was thankful as it meant I only had to make 4 on the last to win by a stroke. I pitched to about $3\frac{1}{2}$ feet and two-putted for the championship. I can remember my friend Henry Longhurst saying, as I went round to tap in the putt, "Be careful, be careful." My score of 71 gave me a total of 278 — a new Open record.

The feeling of walking up the 18th fairway with the gallery surrounding me on both sides and behind will live in my memory forever. To my friend Peter: "Thank you." And to Arnie: "Sorry."

Winning the Open opened lots of doors — invites to the Masters and U.S. Open for five years and lots of years for the championship. I never made the money the boys make today, but I am happy to have won.

To all my fans at St. Andrews and Troon (where I finished a distant second to Palmer in the 1961 Open): "Thank you for the memories."

♦

"Winning the Open opened lots of doors..."

♦

1955

Australian Peter Thomson made his mark as a champion golfer throughout the world. He has won national opens in nine different countries. On the U.S. Senior PGA Tour, Thomson won a record nine tournaments in 1985. His British titles include five Opens during the 1950s and '60s and the 1988 British PGA Seniors. Thomson has his own golf course design firm and recently completed a new course at Craigtoun Park, near St. Andrews.

THE HEART AND SOUL OF GOLF

by Peter Thomson

I first came to St. Andrews two months after winning my first British Open Championship — in 1954, at Royal Birkdale. It was to pay homage to the birthplace of golf and do battle in the British PGA Matchplay Championship. I had not been so far north before during three visits to Britain in the previous three years. I had wanted to go but something inside stopped me. What if it turned out a disappointment? What if all those boyhood dreams were dashed in a discovery that the "holy shrine" was nothing more than a hoax? I needed goading.

So it was that I drove along the winding road into town with Harry Weetman beside me, fresh from an exhibition match in Glasgow. The "auld grey toun," the seven-time Ryder Cup player kept repeating, letting it roll off his tongue.

September is the best time to go. The air is soft and the light subdued. As I gazed down the fairway from the R & A, I felt a lump in my throat. It was all there, just as I had imagined, only more heavenly, more awesome. I was humbled by its majesty.

A day or so later, I was taken by two friends named John — Caithness and Kinnear — to the Rotary lunch, where I heard their version of the game's beginnings. Nothing in print or painting confirms it, yet I accepted it as plausible and have said so ever since.

"St. Andrews," spoke John Caithness, "was once a thriving center of trade as well as religion, particularly with the Low Countries. Dutch ships came, and because this town is high on its bluff, they anchored and came ashore at the end of the links in the Eden.

"They took to walking the long track up to the town steps belting a pebble from the beach with some sort of stick, counting as they went. As the counting got too high they would 'hole out' at six stages into a rabbit scrape or such, on some flat place. And they did the same thing going back again."

"But those sailors were Dutch. How did the locals get involved?" I asked.

"The locals took them on and matches started until the whole town got hooked," he answered. "That was 400 years ago. We're still at it!"

And not only the townsfolk — the whole world is at it. It was the Scots, with a few men from St. Andrews, who took the game to Australia in the 1800s. I'm grateful they did. But back to Fife.

However one judges St. Andrews, as the game's great arena or just a tourist town, it satisfies everyone's dreams. (I know Edinburgh families who journey there each year for the sun and beach, ignoring the golf!) And of course, there is the university, teaching among other things, that unique Scottish law.

Most of all though, it's always been a golfer's mecca. With golf now played worldwide, the game could hardly hold together without the hub in St. Andrews — its heart and soul.

Nowhere can this be felt more that once every seven years or so when the Open rota comes around to the Old Course. Most golfers are thrilled to see the Championship played there. And for those competitors who aspire to the game's highest honors, to take part and perhaps win the Open at the "home of golf" would be, for most of us, the ultimate dream.

The Open Championship there is an occasion of great moment. What always lingers in my memory is the late twilight after the play is done, and the links are crowded with people who witnessed the day's events. They walk gingerly across the greens in their coats and bonnets, stopping here and there to go through the putt that the champion holed or missed. No one shoos them off. There is no need.

Where else in this world could it happen?

Thomson's record of five British Open victories ties him with James Braid, J.H. Taylor and Tom Watson behind the record-setting six of Harry Vardon.

♦

"It was the Scots who took the game to Australia...I'm grateful they did."

♦

1946

Longevity…Who else besides Sam Snead has consistently broken par in seven different decades? His 135-plus tournament victories include three PGA Championships, three Masters and the 1946 British Open.

E S S A Y

MY SCOTTISH CONNECTION
by Sam Snead

When I was a boy of about 7, growing up in the mountains of Virginia, someone gave Pop, my dad, some old iron clubheads made by Tom Stewart of St. Andrews. Knowing that I liked sports, Pop gave them to me. I cut some old broken buggy whips down for shafts and started beating balls around our cow pasture. A few years later, I carved some hickory shafts and put them in the iron heads. Those were the first real clubs I ever had.

It wasn't unusual for a shaft to break off in the head. To get the wood stub out of the head, I would build a fire and burn out the broken shaft. Then I'd carve a new end on the good piece of shaft and attach it to the head. Needless to say, my clubs eventually got too short to use.

My childhood clubmaking proved good experience. When I landed my first assistant pro job at the Homestead Hotel in Hot Springs, Virginia, part of my job, besides giving lessons, was putting together hickory-shafted clubs. Even now, I still have many old clubs. (My son, Jack, has two old long-nose clubs made by former British Open champions Old Tom Morris and Bob Martin.)

In 1946, I traveled overseas to play in the British Open at St. Andrews. As I was taking the train from Edinburgh to St. Andrews, I looked out the window and saw what I thought was a run-down golf course. The bunkers were unraked and shaggy, and some of the boundary fences were falling down. I asked a Scotsman sitting beside me, "What is that course?"

"It's the Old Course, home of the Royal and Ancient," replied the old Scotsman. You could tell he was very proud of it by the way he spoke. I told him that I was traveling from the United States to play on that course. When he learned that I was playing in the Open, he remarked "Aye, the Championship you mean!"

I won that year and enjoyed playing the Old Course very much. You know, over here in the States, we play a lot of target golf where you have to hit high shots with a lot of spin into greens which hold the ball. But on British links courses, you have to play what I call "bounce-in" shots because of the very hard and fast greens. It is something you definitely have to adjust to and, fortunately, I adapted. I especially remember driving the ball very well. In fact, I drove the 10th hole three out of four rounds.

Putting also seemed to be on my side that year. I was using a Tom Stewart blade putter which I had coincidentally taken back to its birthplace. After being made in St. Andrews, the putter was exported to America, where I bought it. Then I took it with me in 1946, so it has crossed the Atlantic three times. I still have it in my personal collection.

The only other British Open I played in was in 1937 at Carnoustie. In two of the rounds I never used a putter! There was so much water on the greens that I had to use a 2-iron and chip to the hole.

Winning the Open at St. Andrews meant a lot to me. I had always heard of it, dreamed of seeing and playing it, realizing it was the home of golf, but never thought that an "ol' country boy" out of the hills of Virginia would someday travel across the Atlantic and win it! Sadly, though, I never played in it again.

My travel expenses were about $2,700 and first prize was only $600. Money was hard to come by in those days, so not many Americans could afford the lengthy trip.

I'm in my 80s now, but still love to play and compete. I seldom shoot over par and just the other day had eight birdies in one round. I wish there were some way to start all over again with today's equipment and prize money. I might even use that old Stewart putter — my St. Andrews connection — for good luck.

A straw hat and a well-balanced swing: two unmistakable trademarks of Sam Snead.

◆

The Old Course played so difficult in the first post war Open, that Snead's high score of 71-70-74-75–290 was good enough for a four-shot victory.

◆

119

1964
TONY LEMA

Arnold Palmer's decision not to play in the 1964 Open certainly benefited Tony Lema. Palmer, champion in 1961 and '62, chose not to play in 1964 because of his hectic schedule. Lema had won four tournaments on the U.S. PGA Tour that year and without Palmer in the field, his chances of winning the Open were greatly improved. Palmer also helped Lema by recommending that he hire Tip Anderson, the caddie responsible for Palmer's wins in Great Britain. As it turned out, Lema would need as much local knowledge as possible, especially with only a couple of days of practice over the Old Course. It was so windy on the first day of the championship that some of the world's best players required woods to reach the first green, normally a short iron. High scores prevailed over first two days, but Lema, by virtue of his lucky draw of starting times, was able to avoid the brunt of the winds. He forged a two-stroke lead at the halfway point. On the final day, Lema held off a determined Jack Nicklaus who shot a course-record 66 in the morning round. Lema's consistent play continued, and he won by five strokes over Nicklaus and six over Roberto DeVicenzo. True to his nickname of "Champagne" Tony, the champion celebrated amid the sounds of corks popping. The following year, Lema returned to Great Britain for the Ryder Cup and to defend his title at the Open, where he finished just four strokes back. Sadly, Lema died in the summer of 1966 in an airplane crash.

1957
BOBBY LOCKE

1939
RICHARD BURTON

The favorites going into the 1957 Open were South African Bobby Locke, with three Open titles to his credit, and thrice defending champion Peter Thomson. American Cary Middlecoff, winner of the Masters and U.S. Open, was also a crowd pleaser. But it was Locke, known for his trademark white cap and plus fours, who would prevail in the first Open to feature live television coverage. After leading the on-site qualifying, he fought off challenges by Thomson and Eric Brown, the noted Scottish professional, who shared the first-round lead with St. Andrean Laurie Ayton with record-tying 67s. Middlecoff never posed a threat. Locke's final rounds of 68-70 won him his fourth and final Open by three shots. There was a slight controversy on the last green when Locke failed to replace his ball on the proper spot after marking to allow another player to putt. The Rules Committee, however, decided that the act was merely a technicality and that a two-stroke penalty would not eradicate his lead. So the matter was dropped. Locke, recognized as one of the game's finest putters, also won the national titles of South Africa, New Zealand, Canada, France, Egypt and Switzerland. An honorary member of the R & A, he died in 1987.

In the last Open before World War II, Richard "Dick" Burton prevailed. Burton, born in Lancashire, had won several professional tournaments and played on two Ryder Cup teams, but was not considered a serious threat by the oddsmakers. Henry Cotton, though, was favored, but never posed a threat. The "star" early in the championship was South African teenager Bobby Locke, an early leader in the pre-tournament qualifying rounds whose first round 70 tied him with Burton and two others for the lead in the tournament proper. At the end of the second day, Burton had a two-stroke lead over the field. On the final day, American Johnny Bulla turned in the day's two best rounds and finished early with 292. Burton played steadily and needed to finish par-par to win by a stroke. On 17, then a par 5, he was short of the green in two, hit a nice pitch and conservatively two-putted. A perfect drive on the 18th put him just short of the Valley of Sin. Burton then pitched to about 10 feet. Attempting to safely two-putt, he holed out instead for a birdie and a comfortable margin of victory. After the war, he won a few titles and played in the 1949 Ryder Cup.

◆

St. Andrews has hosted 25 Open Championships, from 1873 to 1995.

◆

121

122

1933

DENNY SHUTE

Denny Shute's journey to Great Britain in 1933 was a return to his roots. His father, also a golf professional, was born in England and immigrated to the United States in the 1890s. American-born Denny took up the game and enjoyed a fine amateur career before turning pro in 1928. His 1933 Open victory came just two weeks after a most disheartening experience: in the Ryder Cup at Southport, England, he three-putted the last hole when the U.S. team needed him to one-putt for a team victory or two-putt for a tie. Then at St. Andrews, his qualifying rounds of 75-81–156 were 17 strokes behind the low qualifier and he barely made the cutoff. But in the championship proper, Shute returned four rounds of even-par 73 to tie fellow American Craig Wood. By winning the playoff 149-154, he clearly had overcome the embarrassment of his Ryder Cup misfortune. Shute's prowess endured as he captured the 1936 and '37 PGA Championships.

1921

JOCK HUTCHISON

Although Jock Hutchison was the first American citizen to win the Open, he was a St. Andrean by birth. He was the longtime professional at the Glen View Club in suburban Chicago (where Laurence Auchterlonie of St. Andrews also served). In the 1921 Open, Hutchison led the qualifiers and then shot a 72 for the low score on the first day of the Championship. His round was highlighted by back-to-back eagles: a hole-in-one on the eighth and a 2 on the par-4 ninth, where he nearly holed his drive. Hutchison's playing partner that day was Bobby Jones, the American teenaged amateur sensation (see page 88). Early on the final day, young Roger Wethered, an Oxford student just at the beginning of an illustrious amateur career, posted superb rounds of 72-71 and became "leader in the clubhouse." Hutchison, meanwhile, skied to 79 in the morning round, but came back with 70 to tie Wethered. In the subsequent playoff, Hutchison shot 74-76 to win handily by nine strokes. The champion was criticized for his use of deep-grooved irons which, although they had been in use for about seven years, were scheduled to be banned following the 1921 Open.

1905/1910

JAMES BRAID

It was the consistent, spectacular play of the tall and skinny Scotsman, "Jimmy" Braid, at the beginning of the century that put him in the same class with J.H. Taylor and Harry Vardon to form "The Triumvirate." Taylor and Vardon each had won three Open Championships by the time Braid, who had competed as an amateur for several years, won his first in 1901. With subsequent Open titles in 1905, '06, '08 and '10, there was no doubt Braid was their equal. At the 1905 Open in St. Andrews, Old Tom, who was just shy of his 84th birthday, served as the first-tee starter for the final time. But he wasn't alone in the 80s, for not a single player broke 80 in the first round! Vardon and Taylor were joint leaders with 80s over the toughened course, but followed with 82 and 85, respectively, in the second round. Braid was at 81-78—159, one stroke behind Rowland Jones of England. On the final day, Jones skied to 87 in the early round, while Braid's consistent 78 gave him the lead. Although he encountered the railroad tracks twice in the finishing holes, Braid's final-round 81 was sufficient for a 5-stroke victory and the highest winning score in 10 years. In the Jubliee Open of 1910, the first round was canceled due to heavy rain. Once underway, the scores were considerably better than in 1905. Willie Smith from nearby Carnoustie, then living in Mexico, led at the halfway point with 77-71—149, with Braid one stroke behind. But Smith and others could not match Braid's steady rounds of 76-73-74-76 for a 299 aggregate and a 4-stroke victory. Braid was a lifelong club pro; he was the first professional at Walton Heath, near London, when it opened in 1904, and remained there until his death in 1950.

1895/1900

J.H. TAYLOR

In 1895, John Henry "J.H." Taylor successfully defended his Open title in the first 72-hole contest at the Old Course. In a final round, played in rainy and flooded conditions, the English professional from Royal North Devon Golf Club at Westward Ho! recorded a fantastic 78 to finish ahead of third-round leader Sandy Herd and Andra Kirkaldy, both local favorites. (On the Monday preceding the championship, Kirkaldy had defeated Taylor in an exhibition match.) Taylor's next Open win in 1900 — he won five in all — was also at St. Andrews. That year, he equaled the course record of 77 in the second round and broke it with a closing round of 75. Thousands of spectators had been following the pairing of Harold Hilton and Harry Vardon, the reigning Amateur and Open titleholders, but refocused their attention when Taylor came down the stretch.

124

♦

In 1950, J.H. Taylor, James Braid and Willie Auchterlonie were elected honorary members of the R & A, thus becoming the first professionals to receive the honor.

♦

1891
HUGH KIRKALDY

1888
JACK BURNS

Despite a controversy regarding his scorecard, Jack Burns was declared Champion Golfer for 1888. Originally from St. Andrews, he represented Warwick Golf Club, where he was greenkeeper and golf professional. His score of 171 was one less than noted clubmakers David Anderson Jr. of St. Andrews and Bernard Sayers of North Berwick. In the ensuing years, Burns faded from the golf scene and purportedly became a construction worker on the railway.

In the last year that the Open Championship was played in a single day, Hugh Kirkaldy recorded a pair of 83s to edge out his older brother, Andra, and Troon professional Willie Fernie by two strokes. Andra could have tied for first by taking nine strokes over the final two holes, but instead took 11. However, he did win a playoff the following day for second-place honors, for a repeat of his performance in the 1879 Open, also at St. Andrews. It's interesting that of the 61 competitors whose scores appear in the record book, 28 represented St. Andrews clubs, including the winner, who was a member of St. Andrews Golf Club.

1882

BOB FERGUSON

126

Bob Ferguson of Musselburgh won his third Open title in succession in 1882. He shot 83-88–171 to win a cash prize of £11 and a gold medal; his club retained possession of the championship cup for another year. Jamie Anderson, Bob Martin and Willie Fernie, all former or future champions, finished a few strokes behind. In fact, Ferguson would tie with Fernie the following year, only to lose the playoff. Shortly thereafter, Ferguson contracted typhoid and never regained his form. He spent the remainder of his career as a caddie and greenkeeper in Musselburgh.

1879

JAMIE ANDERSON

Recognized as one of the most consistent professional golfers in the late 19th century, Jamie Anderson won his third Open Championship in a row in 1879. Anderson was a member of the well-known St. Andrews family of golfers; his father, Old Da', was a legendary caddie and his brother David ran a successful clubmaking business. Anderson's first round 84 was two ahead of 19-year-old Andra Kirkaldy and his final aggregate of 169 was three ahead of Kirkaldy and Jamie Allan, the Scot playing out of Royal North Devon Golf Club. Kirkaldy, who would later become honorary professional to the R & A, won the playoff match for second place by one stroke the following day.

1876/1885
BOB MARTIN

Bob Martin of St. Andrews captured his two Open titles on his home course. In 1876, Martin was tied with Davie Strath, a professional from St. Andrews then playing out of North Berwick. Both had identical scores of 86-90–176. But Strath was so perturbed about a ruling regarding his approach to the 35th hole hitting into the group ahead that he refused to participate in a playoff for the title. Accordingly, Martin was declared champion. His other title was gained "fair and square" in 1885 with a score of 84-87–171 for a one-shot win over Archie Simpson of Carnoustie. Martin was a clubmaker by profession and worked for many years in Tom Morris' shop.

1873
TOM KIDD

After contesting the first 12 Open Championships at Prestwick, it was decided to begin a rotation of venues in 1873, with the links of St. Andrews and Musselburgh as the added sites. When the top players gathered in St. Andrews that year for the first time to determine who would be the champion golfer, tournament golf was still in its infancy; in fact, the world of golf was so small that of the 21 players whose scores were recorded, 16 were playing from golf clubs based in St. Andrews. Not surprisingly, the top-three finishers were St. Andreans; Tom Kidd won with 91-88–179, Jamie Anderson was one shot back and Young Tom Morris, winner of the four previous Opens, was four off the lead. Kidd, like his father before him, was a caddie in St. Andrews and was recognized as an adept golf instructor.

LOVE AFFAIR WITH THE OLD COURSE PAYS OFF IN VICTORY

by Richard Siderowf

A stockbroker from Connecticut, Dick Siderowf is an experienced competitor outside the United States. His titles include the 1971 Canadian Amateur, and a pair of British Amateurs: in 1973 at Royal Porthcawl in Wales and in 1976 at St. Andrews. He competed in the Walker Cup four times and was captain one time.

The first time I saw St. Andrews was in 1974. I had won the British Amateur Championship the previous year and was defending my title at Muirfield. I had just completed an early morning match, and since my next match wasn't until 4 p.m. the next day, I had a lot of time to kill. So I decided to take the nearly two-hour ride up to St. Andrews.

As soon as I saw the church spires appear on the horizon, I began to get excited about visiting the historic town. Although I had just planned to sight-see, I got an irresistible urge to play golf when I drove by the R & A clubhouse. I signed up at the starters house, paid the green fee of about $4 and waited to be placed into a foursome.

I was put with just two people, who were carrying their own bags. (I had a caddie). We introduced ourselves and off we went. As we finished teeing off on the second hole, a man came out of the Old Course Hotel to join us. It turned out that he was the hotel chef and brother-in-law of one of my playing partners. Perhaps out of respect for the hallowed ground we were walking over, there was little conversation among us except about the course. After the round, we shook hands and went separate ways — the other three never realizing I was the holder of the Amateur title.

The following year I returned to St. Andrews as a member of the U.S. Walker Cup team and stayed at the Old Course Hotel. The chef, my playing partner from the year before, recognized me at one of the buffets and we became "new best friends."

Playing from the championship tees made a world of difference, particularly with a great caddie: Andy Simpson. He knew every bunker by name and where to aim when the wind conditions changed. I got to know the course well and the more I played, the more I wanted to play it again. Although I didn't play particularly well in the Walker Cup, I enjoyed every minute of it.

In 1976, the Amateur Championship was scheduled for St. Andrews. When I sent in my entry, my wife was not thrilled about my going. "You've won the thing once," she said. "Isn't that enough?"

My response was: "This is the last chance I'll have to play at St. Andrews in the Amateur while I'm still playing decently, so I'm going to go." (After reaching the semifinals the previous year and losing to Vinny Giles on the 21st hole, I was determined to capture the title once more.)

My determination paid off — but just barely. In nearly every match I was one or two down with six holes to play, but somehow wiggled off the hook. Two of the matches, including the finals, even went extra holes! A highlight of the victory was to receive the trophy from Joe Dey, the captain of the R & A that year, a man for whom I had the utmost respect.

St. Andrews remains a very special place for me. I have been fortunate to have been a member of the R & A since 1980 and am most anxious to participate in a Spring or Autumn Meeting.

1976

RICHARD SIDEROWF

American Dick Siderowf accepts the Amateur Championship trophy from Joe Dey, captain of the R & A and fellow countryman. The silver trophy is topped with a small figurine of Old Tom Morris.

129

1958

The best record in Irish amateur golf clearly belongs to Joe Carr. From the late 1940s through the 1960s, Carr won dozens and dozens of titles in Ireland and Britain. He was British Amateur champion three times, winning one each in England, Scotland and Ireland. Carr's 10 appearances as a Walker Cup player is a record number for either side.

SUCCESS AT ST. ANDREWS

by Joe Carr

I have been asked what St. Andrews means to me. I have had a love affair with St. Andrews since I first played there in 1947 in the first post war Walker Cup match. I was lucky enough to play and beat the American champion, Ted Bishop. Over the following years in St. Andrews, I held the record for both the Old and New courses simultaneously, won the Amateur in 1958, and had a great chance of winning the Centenary Open in 1960. I watched my son Roddy there in 1971 on the winning Walker Cup team, led by my great friend Michael Bonallack, and a decade later, my son John made it to the semifinals in the Amateur. You can well imagine how much I love this golf course.

I have been fortunate enough over the years to receive many awards: the Bob Jones Award, Walter Hagen Award, Golden Tee Award and Golf Writers Trophy. Then in 1991, at a stage when I thought acclaim was a thing of the past, the greatest honor of all was bestowed on me: I was elected captain of the world-renowned and respected institution, the Royal and Ancient Golf Club of St. Andrews. I am very proud to add my name to the list of distinguished predecessors.

To use Bobby Jones' own words, "If I had to play golf on any one course for the rest of my life, my choice would be the Old Course. I have played the course many hundreds of times, and I have never yet found it anything but different." These are my sentiments exactly.

But there is something deeper for all of us who love golf, who value sportsmanship, friendship, traditions and standards. St. Andrews is the source and inspiration.

I come from an island that is tragically flawed by violence, yet the difference of religious beliefs or political aspirations that underlie that violence stop magically on the first tee of every golf club in Ireland — North and South. All of us who play have developed friendships over many years that accommodate and respect different views, and transcend borders and barriers.

Based on my experience on the potential our game has to bring people of all creeds and colors together, it is my hope that my captaincy of the R & A, in some small way, focused attention on golf as an international language of peace and friendships.

1981

PHILIPPE PLOUJOUX

The 1981 Amateur win by 26-year-old Frenchman Philippe Ploujoux was the first ever by a golfer from the Continent. Spectators marveled as the stocky Parisian sent down opponents with his putting wizardry. In the finals, he defeated American Joel Hirsch — who turned 40 during the championship — by a score of 4 & 2. The semifinal rounds were an international affair: Ploujoux beat Irishman John Carr, son of the famous amateur Joe Carr (see page 130), while Hirsch defeated Tony Gresham of Australia. Ploujoux, once a successful junior golfer, accepted his two automatic invitations to play in the Masters, then redirected his efforts to a career in the golf goods business. Hirsch, a resident of Chicago, has won numerous regional competitions and continues to compete in the Amateur and also the British Senior Open.

1963

MICHAEL LUNT

After Joe Carr, Michael Bonallack and Ronnie Shade were eliminated in early matches, 28-year-old English Walker Cup player Michael Lunt made his way into the finals of the 1963 Amateur. His opponent was John Blackwell, a member of the R & A from Sandwich. The quality of play in the first round of their match was far from stellar as bogies and double-bogies proliferated. But neither player dominated and the match was all even. In the afternoon, Lunt was 2-up after nine holes. He found trouble on the 14th and had to pick up, losing to a bogey, but held on to win 2 & 1. Lunt reached the finals the following year, but lost on the 39th hole. In 1966, he won the English Amateur.

1950

FRANK STRANHAN

American Frank Stranahan was no stranger to British championship golf when he arrived in St. Andrews for the 1950 Amateur; he had won the 1948 Amateur and was runner-up in the 1947 Open. But at the beginning of the event, the gallery's attention was not directed toward Stranahan or even the legendary Francis Ouimet. Everyone wanted to see Bing Crosby, the entertainer, play golf. Crosby played well in the qualifier and birdied two of the first three holes in his first round match before losing 3 & 2. In his quest for another title, Stranahan got revenge over Sam McCready of Ireland, the defending champion, who had defeated him in a match a year earlier in the championship at Portmarnock. Once in the finals, Stranahan was 3-up at the break, then won five of the next 12 holes for an 8 & 6 victory over fellow American Dick Chapman. Chapman persisted, however, and returned to capture the Amateur the next year. Stranahan nearly won another British title in 1953, finishing second in the Open at Carnoustie to Ben Hogan. He turned pro in 1954, but never won another major.

1936

HECTOR THOMSON

132

Hector Thomson was the son of a Scottish professional and enjoyed a fine amateur career before turning professional in 1940. Prior to his victory in the Amateur, he had won the British Boy's, the Irish Open Amateur and the Scottish Amateur (at St. Andrews). At the 1936 Amateur in St. Andrews, there were several experienced contenders, such as Cyril Tolley, Roger Wethered and Jock McLean. But it was youth that prevailed, as Thomson and Australian Jim Ferrier, both in their early 20s, reached the finals. Playing in rain and hail, Thomson rallied from 3-down in the morning to 2-up at the afternoon turn. He was 2-up with two to play when Ferrier birdied the 17th to stay in the match. But after Thomson nearly holed out his approach for an eagle at the 18th, Ferrier conceded the birdie, and the match. Thomson later turned pro and held jobs in Greece, Egypt, Switzerland and Italy. Ferrier was just at the onset of a successful golfing career. (He would later win the 1947 PGA Championship.)

1924

ERNEST HOLDERNESS

The 1924 Amateur Championship was the second for Ernest Holderness; he won in 1922 at Prestwick. Holderness was born in India, played for the Oxford University golf team and was a three-time Walker Cupper (including the 1923 match, played at St. Andrews). His opponent in the final match was E.F. Storey, the 23-year-old captain of the Cambridge University team. Storey had defeated Roger Wethered, the titleholder, in his march to the championship round. In the final match, Storey started with a birdie and was 4-up after 11. Holderness whittled the lead to 1-up after 18 holes, then went ahead by one at the fourth in the afternoon. Holderness played steadily through the cold and rain and finally closed out the match on the 16th, 3 & 2.

1907

JOHN BALL

With John Ball Jr. winning the Amateur Championship a record eight times, between 1888 and 1912, it is no surprise that he claimed a victory at St. Andrews. The draw resulted in a first-round pairing worthy of a championship final: Ball and Johnny Laidlay, two of the game's top amateurs. Ball, playing from Royal Liverpool, won 3 & 1 amid spectacular scoring; the duo's best ball was 1-under 4s for the 17 holes. Ball survived six more matches to reach the finals against C.A. Palmer, a member of the R & A, who was playing his home course. The rain and wind were so severe that the best medal score in the morning round of the 36-hole match was a 90 by Ball. Despite the continued rain in the afternoon, 2,000 spectators followed the match and saw Ball win 6 & 5. The presentation ceremony was conducted by captain of the R & A, and former Amateur Champion, Leslie Balfour-Melville. The captain had been a contestant that year, losing in the third round. Ball's victories included the 1890 Open Championship, becoming both the first amateur and first Englishman to do so.

1901/1913

HAROLD HILTON

Typical of the great British amateur golfers of a century ago, Harold Hilton could hold his own against the professionals. Ironically, he won two Open Championships, in 1892 and '97, prior to winning his first of four Amateur Championships in 1900. In 1911, Hilton wore both the British and U.S. Amateur crowns. (No other British golfer has since won the U.S. title.) The stocky Englishman was born near Hoylake and played out of the Royal Liverpool Golf Club. In the 1901 Amateur at St. Andrews, he defeated John L. Low on the 36th hole. Low, a Scotsman, was longtime chairman of the Rules of Golf Committee and a prolific writer on the game. (He and Hilton co-authored Concerning Golf *in 1903.) At the 1913 Amateur, John Ball, the defending champion and Hilton's lifelong friend, was forced to withdraw due to injuries from a motorcycle accident. This left Hilton as the lone favorite. After several close matches, including two ending in sudden death, Hilton regained his form to handily win the 36-hole finals against Robert Harris (who would eventually win the championship in 1925). Hilton was a golf writer as well. He wrote an autobiography,* My Golfing Reminiscences, *and paired with Garden Smith to write the elegant and classic* The Royal and Ancient Game of Golf.

134

1895

LESLIE BALFOUR-MELVILLE

From 1874 to 1908, Leslie Balfour-Melville won numerous medals at both the R & A and St. Andrews golf clubs. He was runner-up to John Laidlay in the 1889 Amateur on the Old Course, so his win in the 1895 event was not a total surprise. It was not an easy win, though. Three of his matches went 19 holes, including the final one against the great John Ball, winner of four Amateur titles at that time. Balfour-Melville was elected captain of the R & A in 1906 and had been captain of the Honourable Company of Edinburgh Golfers in 1902-3. In addition to golf, he excelled at rugby, cricket and lawn tennis.

1889/1891

JOHN LAIDLAY

Johnny Laidlay won well over a hundred significant golf medals at St. Andrews, Musselburgh, North Berwick and Prestwick. He was a member of the R & A and the Honourable Company. Laidlay's two victories in the Amateur Championship were at St. Andrews. In 1889, he beat Leslie Balfour-Melville and in 1891, he defeated Harold Hilton on the first extra hole. He also was runner-up in the Amateur in 1888 and '90, and in 1893 finished second in both the Open and the Amateur. Laidlay was one of the first to use the overlapping grip, years before it was popularized by Harry Vardon. And in putting, he went a step further by overlapping his entire right hand over the left one.

1886

HORACE HUTCHINSON

After losing in the finals of the inaugural Amateur Championship in 1885, Horace Hutchinson won the next two. In 1886 at St. Andrews, he quickly disposed of Henry Lamb in the 18-hole final match by a score of 7 & 6. Hutchinson was a prominent golf writer. His book credits include Golf: The Badminton Library and Fifty Years of Golf. Born in London, Hutchinson was raised near Royal North Devon Golf Club, where a young J.H. Taylor, the future golf champion, sometimes caddied for him. Hutchinson played his way into captaincy there, when at the age of 16, he won the club's Autumn Meeting; later in life, he was elected president. Hutchinson also was made captain at Royal St. George's, Royal Liverpool and the Royal and Ancient.

Many of the top amateur golfers of the late 19th century — John Ball, Johnny Laidlay, Harold Hilton, Horace Hutchinson and Freddie Tait — could hold their own against the professionals.

SCIENCE AND GOLF IN VICTORIAN DAYS

by Margaret Tait

Miss Margaret Tait is the niece of golf champion Freddie Tait. Now in her 80s, she resides in St. Andrews, but considers Edinburgh her genuine home. Her father, John Guthrie Tait (Freddie's brother), was a classical scholar who spent much of his career as a college educator in India.

I am flattered at being asked to write an article for a book called *St. Andrews & Golf*, for I am neither a St. Andrean nor a golfer. I imagine that because I've been sharing information about the Tait family with Morton Olman for nearly 20 years, he felt that it would be appropriate for me to comment on my ancestors. My grandfather, Professor Peter Guthrie Tait, was a prominent scientist and my uncle, Frederick Guthrie Tait, won the Amateur Championship on two occasions. Although they both died before I was born, I feel as if I knew them from reading their scrapbooks and reminiscing with family members.

My grandfather was known more often as P.G., "the Professor" or Guthrie (his grandmother's maiden name), rather than by his first name. He was born in 1831 in Dalkeith, and educated in nearby Edinburgh. After serving for a time as professor of mathematics at the University of Queens College in Belfast, P.G. Tait returned to the University of Edinburgh in 1860, where he was Professor of Natural Philosophy until his death in 1901. A few years before the birth of Freddie — his sixth child — in 1870, friends recommended St. Andrews as a healthy holiday place for families with children.

St. Andrews remained the Tait summer home for many years as the family enjoyed sea-bathing and golf. The Professor had learned to play golf on the Bruntsfield Links about a decade earlier and was a member of the Honourable Company of Golfers when it played at Musselburgh. He also became a member of the Royal and Ancient, and was known to play several rounds in a day, often starting at 6 a.m. The Professor was fascinated with more than just playing golf: it was while waiting at the starter's box in 1887, that he got his idea to study the flight of the golf ball, as he listened to caddies talking about the wind. His famous writings appeared in both golf and scholarly journals, and helped golfers better understand why their shots sometimes went crooked.

His sons also enjoyed golf. My father, John Guthrie Tait — known as Jack — was the oldest of the four sons. He was a good golfer, having made it to the fourth round of the 1901 Amateur Championship, which was held at the Old Course. But it was Uncle Freddie who made such a great showing during the 1890s. He won the Amateur Championship in 1896 and 1898, and was runner-up in 1899. He twice finished in third place at the Open Championship and also won many of the medals at the R & A. Freddie had much military training as a young man and attained the rank of lieutenant in the Black Watch. He was at the prime of his golf game in the autumn of 1899, when his regiment was ordered to duty in the war in South Africa; Freddie died in action the following February.

Freddie's father, Peter Guthrie Tait, was an eminent professor at the University of Edinburgh. He was particularly interested in the physics of golf ball flight. His extensive research and experiments in the 1880s and '90s are recognized as the first scientific analyses of the game. Tait's life was recounted in Life and Scientific Work of Peter Guthrie Tait, *written by C.G. Knott in 1911. The Tait home at 17 Drummond Place in Edinburgh (where Freddie was born) is now Drummond House, an elegant guest house.*

Freddie Tait, Amateur champion of 1896 and 1898, was a member of the R & A. During the 1890s, he competed against a formidable group of amateurs, including John Ball, John Laidlay, Horace Hutchinson and Harold Hilton. His promising career was cut short in 1900, at the age of 30, when he was fatally wounded in the Boer War.

138

When he sailed for military duty in South Africa, Tait left Nails, his canine companion, in the care of his parents. In letters sent home from the battlefield, Lt. Tait often closed with a reminder to give the terrier "a bone with plenty of meat on it." After Tait was killed in battle, a "letter" from Nails — complete with pawprint — was found in a pocket of his uniform.

◆

"The Professor was loved for his wonderful sense of humor, and his son Freddie was admired for his friendliness and bright outlook on life."

— Margaret Tait

◆

At 6 years of age, Tait already knew how to handle a golf club. This drawing was taken from a picture by Thomas Rodger, the noted St. Andrews photographer.

REFLECTIONS ON THE OLD COURSE

by Sir Henry Cotton

The following text appeared in Golf Illustrated *in 1954.*

One thing I learned as a young golfer was that a good golf course does not have to look like a golf course to be good. I mean that the holes do not have to be photogenic to be great. This is so true when one visits St. Andrews, for the ground looks so flat to the eye that it looks dull.

You never begin by liking the Old Course, and the atmosphere seems a bit unfriendly at first. The bay window of the old stone clubhouse is generally crowded with critical golfers all reliving the great days of the past and, you can feel, criticizing your swing as you play your opening drive or the final strokes on the 18th.

When you get to know those old boys, you find they are just golfers like yourself, a shade older maybe, but just lovers of the game and upholders of our heritage.

I have lost a couple of Open Championships there after getting into a decent winning position. I say lost, but I suppose that is a bit of an exaggeration, though once I tried for the lead with one round to go. I finished three strokes behind because my ball finished on a severe upslope on the 13th fairway coming back against the strong wind, and I tried to gain distance by forcing the shot.

I've done everything at St. Andrews in major events — popped one into the Swilcan Burn before the first green; been in the deep bunker at the 11th and had an impossible lie…I've been out of bounds at the 14th over the wall when 7-under-4s and going like a dream to crash with a 7 for the hole. I've been, of course, in Hell Bunker with a second shot which just failed to make it. At the 16th I've been in the "Principal's Nose" and dropped another shot… I've been — oh dear! — 3-under on the 17th tee several times and then hit one onto the road.

I think (the 18th) hole is one of the greatest in the world — so easy yet so terrible. And to wind up I've three-putted the 18th green from the hollow AND alas! from the flat top, before the thousands of locals too, and then one creeps off the green feeling about knee high — nothing more humbling in this world. In fact, St. Andrews teaches humility.

Henry Cotton — champion golfer, teacher, author and golf course architect — did so much to improve the quality of the game in Britain that he became the first to achieve knighthood for his contributions to golf. Sadly, he died in 1987, shortly before the public announcement of his recognition. Cotton won the Open in 1934, '37 and '48, during a period of 75 years when no Briton held the title more than once. Although he was at his competitive prime in the late 1920s and 1930s, he continued to win an occasional tournament after the war. Cotton's biography, Maestro: The Life of Henry Cotton, *was written after his death by Peter Dobereiner.*

I feel that my small repayment to St. Andrews for the pleasure I have had has been to suggest that the Old Course become an arena with the spectators watching play from the outside. This I proposed in an article just before the war — I took an aerial photo and drew in the grandstands and crossovers. Part of the plan was carried out successfully, and I am proud of the letter of appreciation I had from the R & A for my suggestion. Overnight, the Old Course, far from becoming obsolete from a crowd control angle, became the most modern golfing arena in the world. A model course, almost!

"Chickie" Moss, Cotton's step-daughter, has a keen interest in golf and often attends major golf events.

I do not get cross anymore when young golfers claim they detest the place, I just feel sorry they are so ignorant and unappreciative of what they have inherited — but I am sure most of these, as they grow older, learn to understand that golf is a dull game when every hole plays the same way every day. At St. Andrews you never know what to expect.

I cannot say more than I just love the place.

Contemporaries Henry Cotton (left) and Gene Sarazen competed against each other in the Ryder Cup and major championships, but their most memorable meeting was a match over the Old Course in 1961 that was filmed for the television show, "Shell's Wonderful World of Golf." After a battle against not only each other, but also strong winds and rain, Sarazen emerged the victor.

142

Lady Heathcoat-Amory, or Miss Joyce Wethered, as she was known during her competitive days, was Britain's top female golfer in the 1920s.

Bobby Jones remarked after an exhibition in 1930 that she was the finest ball-striker he had ever seen — man or woman. She won four British Ladies' Amateur Championships, the English Ladies' Championship five times in succession, and many mixed foursome titles.

In 1925, at the age of 24, Wethered retired from competition. But the lure of the Ladies' Championship at St. Andrews in 1929 brought her out of retirement. She reached the finals, and after the first nine holes of the morning round found herself 5-down to Glenna Collett, the American champion. Not unexpectedly, Wethered battled back to win the match on the 35th hole for her fourth victory in the championship.

Upon marriage to Sir John Heathcoat-Amory in 1937, she became Lady Heathcoat-Amory. (While on honeymoon in Bermuda, the newlyweds enjoyed a round of golf with American Joe Dey — then executive secretary of the USGA and a future captain of the R & A — who also was honeymooning).

After retiring from competitive golf, Lady Heathcoat-Amory became an avid horticulturist.

THE OLD COURSE: "I LOVE EVERY HUMMOCK..."

by Lady Heathcoat-Amory

The following recollections are excerpted from Golfing Memories and Methods *by Joyce Wethered, published in 1933.*

What a joy it is to jump into the train in the evening at a London terminus, with one's clubs on the rack overhead, and to wake the next morning to the sounds of Edinburgh and then the strange hum of the train rumbling over the Forth Bridge. ...

It is a journey as full of charm and interest as the destination we are bound for. The last mile or so runs down the side of the links and the first exciting glimpse of St. Andrews is caught. All too soon the train carries us ahead, wreathing the 17th tee in its smoke as it passes. ...

The first of my many visits was paid a number of years ago [in 1922]. I remember arriving in a state of considerable excitement as to what my first impressions would be. I had, of course, garnered certain ideas about the course, as only the year before my brother had tied for the Open Championship on it. I must admit that my first sight of the Valley of Sin, into which Roger's ball fell in the last round (costing him a five and the championship) caused me a sense of acute disappointment. It was pointed out to me from the window of the Hotel — a small, uninspiring hollow, to be the cause of such an unhappy ending. I could not help inwardly hoping that Hell Bunker and the famous 11th hole would come nearer to my grim expectations.

Driving from the first tee on the following morning, I remember I was not altogether free from terror. My knees were inclined to be unsteady; the tee seemed a vast and empty space, and my ball and myself very small and insignificant in the middle of it. To make things more disturbing still, the large plate glass window in the club room overlooking us was filled with faces. My brother more than once that morning had called my attention to the fountain to the right of the fairway, and I knew that the object of his remarks was to inveigle me into hitting it, or at any rate drifting in that direction. However, I saw plenty of room to the left and managed to pull a low drive into a region of safety. The second shot happened to be a long one that day and I barely carried the Swilken Burn with a brassie. I wondered whether it would be my fate every morning to make this perilous shot.

By the fourth hole I was completely befogged, lost and bewildered. On the last course I had played on, the greens and the bottom of the pin stared comfortably at me. Here I seemed fortunate if I could catch a glimpse of the top of the flag. Certainly so far, except for the first hole, I had not yet seen any of the greens to which I was approaching.

At this point, resigning to all claims of independence, I delivered myself completely into the hand of my one-armed caddie. For the rest of the round I played obediently over bumps and bunkers, at spires and hotels in the distance, and finally at the 17th hole — with no spirit left to differ or question — over the top of a large shed which clearly belonged to a railway goods yard. At the last hole, to my opponent's evident satisfaction, my ball fell into the Valley of Sin, no doubt a fitting conclusion to a bewildering round.

St. Andrews, I fancy, usually treats a visitor very much in this fashion. At first sight it is almost impossible to grasp the idea of the course. The good drives end in bunkers; the straight approaches run away from the hole; the putts wander all over the greens. To become a genuine lover of St. Andrews needs plenty of time and experience. I stayed a fortnight on my first visit and the last week passed in a flash — one heavenly day after another. It took the whole of the first week to sort out the holes and even to begin to understand the links; but ever since, the Old Course has stood alone in my estimation and I love every hummock of it…

St. Andrews never changes. It is the same every year that one visits it. The holes remain unchanged; the same old characters greet one; the same long stream of townsfolk drive off the first tee when the day's work is finished. As they fade away into the distance over the Swilcan Burn, we cannot but envy them in their inherited possession.

Lady Heathcoat-Amory (née Joyce Wethered) on the first tee of the Old Course. In her six appearances in the British Ladies' Championship, she won 38 matches and lost just two.

144

Gary Player — winner of three Opens, one U.S. Open, three Masters, two U.S. PGAs, three U.S. PGA Seniors, two U.S. Senior Opens and two British Senior Opens — was a pioneer in stressing the benefits of proper diet and exercise for golfers. As a 54-year-old competitor in the 1990 Open in St. Andrews, a handstand was not beyond his means. That Player won his Open titles in three different decades is proof of his durability. He is currently an honorary member of the R & A.

In the 1990 Open, Player was joined by his son Wayne, who made the field through the qualifying rounds. The duo joined an elite group of father/son co-competitors that includes the Willie Parks and Tom Morrisses — four noted ex-champions.

American amateur great Chick Evans plays a shot from the road on the 17th hole in 1911. At the time, he had won numerous amateur titles and the Western Open (then considered a "major"). Evans visited St. Andrews while on a European trip to Prestwick for the British Amateur and to France for the French Amateur Open, which he won. He later won both the U.S. Amateur and U.S. Open in 1916, as well as another U.S. Amateur title in 1920.

♦

"In golf there are no strangers, but only friends you've never met."

— Bill Campbell

♦

John W. (Johnny) Fischer, the 1936 U.S. Amateur champion, played for the American team twice in Walker Cup matches held at the Old Course. In 1934, he won a singles match as the United States won handily. In 1938, Fischer played admirably — winning his singles match and halving in the foursomes — but the Americans fell victims for the first time after winning the first nine contests. (See pages 58-61 for more about the 1938 Walker Cup.)

A STRONGHOLD OF GOLF TRADITION

by Ben Crenshaw

Winner of 19 events on the U.S. Tour, including the 1984 and '95 Masters Tournaments, Texan Ben Crenshaw has earned a top-10 position on the official career earnings list. He has been runner-up in the Open twice and, as an ardent golf historian, would like nothing more than to win this oldest of major championships. Crenshaw has been on the Tour since 1973 and even though he devotes considerable time to designing golf courses, he continues to play his way into the winner's circle.

I wish that every golfer could go to St. Andrews. There is so much history and romance.

St. Andrews is a living testament as to what golf was, how it evolved and what it should be in the future. It is unchanging, proud, dignified and truthful. It can be unkind, unfair and uncompromising. But it also can be thrilling, rewarding, kind and gentle. In a round of golf at St. Andrews, all these experiences are magnified, and these are some of the reasons why golf retains its mystery and fascination, along with its parallels of life's tribulations.

I first visited St. Andrews to play in the 1978 Open Championship. I arrived by helicopter, and I suppose, happily enough, that was a marvelous first look. The weather was bright, and below me spread the "dear old city" with the Old, New, Eden and Jubilee courses, bordered by the prominent Royal and Ancient clubhouse. I was finally there and I couldn't believe it! I had read a lot about St. Andrews and was I excited.

One may study all the maps of the Old Course he likes in order to familiarize himself with the links, but there remains a lifetime of study in really knowing it. Bobby Jones always said that it remained the most fascinating course of all, and I certainly agree. Since the ground itself is an endless sea of undulations, it is only an abiding sense of knowledge about the course that will get you through in the constant breezes.

I must say, I coped pretty well during my first Open at St. Andrews, finishing joint runner-up with Tom Kite, Raymond Floyd and the hapless Simon Owen. Jack Nicklaus outwaited our impatience and killed us off in the end. I had an outgoing 39 in the face of the breeze the last day with an untidy 6 on the Ginger Beer Hole, but I came back in 32 to finish respectably. I remember being paired with my friend Isao Aoki for all four rounds, and between us, we holed some unbelievable putts.

I returned for the 1984 Open, and although I couldn't get my game going too well, I managed a hole-in-one in the final round at the eighth. Making that ace at St. Andrews was one of the highlights of my career! I finished with a 69 — 10 shots back — and watched the television to see Tom Watson valiantly attempt to overtake Seve Ballesteros in the last round. But Tom ended up against the wall at the Road Hole. The resulting 5 was too much at the time, and then Seve made a magnificent 3 on the final hole with a curling 12-foot putt. What a great finish that was with two great champions in full flight. When Seve made that putt at the last and punched the air with his fist like a matador, I jumped right out of my seat.

In 1990, Nick Faldo surgically removed the entire field with astounding accuracy. He played magnificent golf that week with the precision we have all come to know from Nick. I played a solid tee-to-green game, but my putter killed me. I was really disappointed for two reasons: the greens were perfect, and I knew it would be one of the last remaining opportunities for me to win at St. Andrews.

But there are other rewards of a personal nature that I have experienced at St. Andrews. I have been made to feel welcome by total strangers who share the love of St. Andrews and golf. Many people have known that I love studying the history of golf, and I am very proud to continue to learn of its noble heritage. If you will forgive me for an extremely biased opinion, golf is one of the last unspoiled pursuits left in this crazy world of ours. Fortunately, St. Andrews provides all golfers with a time-honored code of etiquette and behavior passed down through the generations. It also prolongs the tradition of simply enjoying the game, whether one is a professional or caddie, young or old, commoner or king.

Even though St. Andrews adopted the first set of rules from the Honourable Company of Edinburgh Golfers, compiled in 1744, it quickly became the recognized home of the game because golf was universally popular there, and it was vitally important to the town itself. Countless golf enthusiasts have played an important role at St. Andrews in fostering this rich tradition and this is why St. Andrews will always be the "home of golf."

Bobby Jones spoke for all golfers when he received the Freedom of the City in 1958 when golfers from many countries gathered at St. Andrews for the inaugural Eisenhower World Team Championships. The Scots loved Jones, not only for the magnificent golfer he was, but for the kind of man they came to know. He was simply their idea of what a champion should be. His affection for St. Andrews was already known, but this time he spoke directly to St. Andrews, and how his triumphs and tragedies there had deeply moved him as a person. His interpretation of the word "friends" in connection with St. Andrews and the making of friends is quite simply the most beautiful thing I have ever heard in connection to golf. Only Bobby Jones could possess the necessary traits to make such a speech possible with exceedingly rare taste and modesty. He truly spoke for all of us who have ever been there and attempted to repay the simple courtesies extended to golfing pilgrims by the people of St. Andrews, who welcome us there and allow us to enjoy what they have enjoyed for some 500 years.

MAJOR GOLF COMPETITIONS HELD IN ST. ANDREWS

ALCAN GOLFER OF THE YEAR
CHAMPIONSHIP
1967, 1968, 1969, 1970

ALCAN INTERNATIONAL
CHAMPIONSHIP
1967, 1968, 1970

ALFRED DUNHILL CUP
1985 TO PRESENT

AMATEUR CHAMPIONSHIP
1886, 1889, 1891, 1895,
1901, 1907, 1913, 1924,
1930, 1936, 1950, 1958,
1963, 1976, 1981

BOYS' AMATEUR CHAMPIONSHIP
1949

LADIES' OPEN AMATEUR
CHAMPIONSHIP
1908, 1929, 1965, 1975

OPEN CHAMPIONSHIP
1873, 1876, 1879, 1882,
1885, 1888, 1891, 1895,
1900, 1905, 1910, 1921,
1927, 1933, 1939, 1946,
1955, 1957, 1960, 1964,
1970, 1978, 1984,
1990, 1995

SCOTTISH AMATEUR
CHAMPIONSHIP
1922, 1935, 1951, 1959,
1965, 1971, 1976

SCOTTISH LADIES'
CHAMPIONSHIP
1911, 1922, 1928, 1950,
1961, 1973, 1986

SCOTTISH OPEN AMATEUR
STROKEPLAY CHAMPIONSHIP
1993

SENIOR OPEN AMATEUR
CHAMPIONSHIP
1972

WALKER CUP
1923, 1926, 1934, 1938,
1947, 1955, 1971,

WORLD AMATEUR TEAM
CHAMPIONSHIP
1958

This view from behind the first green shows how near the Swilcan Burn the hole can be cut.

150

It's only a matter of time before Open patrons need to rest their legs. Perhaps even more exhausting than walking the links is a visit to the monstrous "tented village," a temporary assemblage of the latest in golf equipment, accessories and services. The first time an exhibition tent was erected at a St. Andrews Open was in 1910. It featured about 60 exhibitors and measured 60 by 270 feet. Now the tents cover an area 18 times that size.

Although an elaborate Golf Practice Centre opened in 1993 near the Old Course's 16th hole, the site remains the location of the tented village during the Open. As in the past, Open contestants utilize a temporary driving range near the 18th of the New Course. Here, a worker cleans and sorts the balls during the 1990 Championship.

By employing hundreds of youngsters and other temporary help, rubbish is kept to a minimum on the links.

◆

"...after the play is done... people who witnessed the day's events...walk gingerly across the greens in their coats and bonnets, stopping here and there to go through the putt that the champion holed or missed. No one shoos them off. There is no need."

— Peter Thomson

◆

152

Vantage point from atop the wall along the 14th fairway.

154

Wherever possible, physically challenged spectators are given priority viewing locations.

There's enough temporary grandstand seating at the Open for 18,000 fans. But as soon as tournament play is finished, the dismantling process begins so that the course is ready for regular play.

Some of the best glimpses of golf action are had early during championship week, while the gallery is sparse.

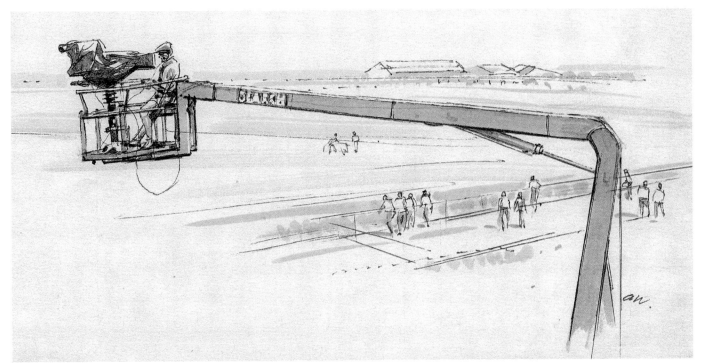

Because the terrain of the Old Course is predominantly flat, television cameras must be mounted on aerial lifts or cranes to give proper perspective.

The dean of British golf announcers is Peter Alliss, who announces for both the BBC and ABC. As a player, he competed in the Ryder Cup eight times and won numerous tournaments in the U.K. and Europe. He once held the professional course record of 66 at the Old Course.

156

Jerry Pate (left), a former U.S. Amateur and U.S. Open champion, and veteran touring pro Ed Sneed (right) have exchanged their golf clubs for microphones. They now provide on-course commentary for ABC Sports.

David Begg, press officer to the Open Champion-ship, conducts player interviews in the press center.

Practice rounds often afford easy access around the course, as depicted here at the fifth green and adjacent sixth tee.

◆

Nearly 1,000 reporters and photographers cover the Open Championship.

◆

158

Throughout the first half of the 20th century, Englishman Bernard Darwin (1876-1961) had few rivals as a golf writer. His style and eloquence brought added beauty to the game in his regular reports for The Times *and* Country Life. *He covered matches and championships on foot, long before the advent of electronic scoring systems and television monitors so popular with writers today. Darwin was an excellent amateur golfer as well; he won several tournaments of note, played in the England vs. Scotland matches for eight years, and was elected captain of the R & A in 1934. His more than 20 books on golf — including* Golf Courses of the British Isles *and his autobiography,* The World That Fred Made — *are treasured by collectors today.*

Texan Dan Jenkins was a newspaper writer before joining Sports Illustrated in 1962. He first was head football writer, then took over the golf beat in 1967. Since 1985, he's covered the majors and special stories for Golf Digest. Jenkins, who attended the same Fort Worth high school as Ben Hogan, has written several golf books, the latest being Fairways and Greens.

George Peper, editor-in-chief of GOLF Magazine since 1979, is an avid golfer. He is a frequent visitor to St. Andrews, where he owns a flat and is an overseas member of the R & A. Peper has written and edited nine books on golf, including the definitive Golf in America and Golf Courses of the PGA Tour.

Kaye Kessler spent nearly all of his 45-year tenure at the Citizen Journal in Columbus, Ohio, in the sports department. As golf writer and columnist, he had the opportunity to witness the development of a talented, local golfer: Jack Nicklaus. Kessler saw Nicklaus go from a 10-year-old participant in a junior clinic to U.S. Amateur and national collegiate champion to become the best golfer of the modern era. He covered many of Nicklaus' victories, including the 1978 Open at St. Andrews. Now semiretired in Colorado, Kessler continues to write about golf on a freelance basis.

Michael Williams has been golf correspondent with The Daily Telegraph since 1971. He authored The Official History of the Ryder Cup and is editor of The Golfer's Handbook.

Ross Goodner retired from Golf Digest in 1993, after 16 years as a senior editor. A respected golf historian, Goodner has written Golf's Greatest and Chicago Golf Club 1892-1992.

160

Alexander Ogilvy Cheape poses in front of his home at Strathtyrum, an estate once encompassing thousands of acres. Cheape, who died in 1981, was the fourth generation of his family to own the land since 1782. It was James Cheape, his great-grandfather's brother and captain of the R & A, who was famous for rescuing the links from destruction by rabbit farmers; he purchased the property in 1821 so that golfers could use it. (Town Council had sold the land in 1797 because it was in such great debt.) In 1894, after a series of transactions, the town regained control of the links. Alexander's father, James, sold the property with several provisions — one granted the Cheape family six daily tee times on the Old Course.

Gladys Cheape, originally from Barbados, married Alexander Ogilvy Cheape in 1952. Now a widow, she continues to oversee the operation of the Strathtyrum estate. In 1992, she transferred the Cheape family's century-old rights of access to the links to the St. Andrews Links Trust. In 1971 and 1986, the family had sold property to the trust for the construction of the Balgove and Strathtyrum golf courses.

One of the conditions of the St. Andrews Links Act of 1894 was that the Cheape family, owners of the links for most of the 19th century, could excavate shells from beneath the golf turf for the purpose of paving the roads of their Strathtyrum estate. Shown here is the removal of sod on the sixth fairway of the Eden Course in 1990 prior to the digging of shells.

Cheape's Bunker comes into play off the tees of the parallel second and 17th holes of the Old Course. Long before the construction of the Old Course Hotel and the sheds before it, and long before stately trees enveloped the Strathtyrum mansion, the Cheape family probably could see the bunker named in their honor from their home overlooking the links.

"THE GOLFERS"

One of golf's most famous paintings, "The Golfers," makes its home at Strathtyrum, the Cheape estate (right). Painted by Charles Lees in 1847 (above), this 7-foot-long scene depicts a famous match from 1844 on the 15th green of the St. Andrews links. Shown are Major Hugh Lyon Playfair and John Campbell against Sir David Baird and Sir Ralph Anstruther, surrounded by townsfolk, with the St. Andrews skyline in the distance.

Lees (1800-1880) was a member of the Royal Scottish Academy and studied under Sir Henry Raeburn. He was a painter of portraits, landscapes and historical scenes, and combined all three elements in "The Golfers." Prior to creating the final work, he executed numerous small studies of the nearly 60 identifiable characters; several appear as color plates in *A History of the Royal and Ancient Golf Club* by H.S.C. Everard. In 1850, the painting was reproduced as an engraving. Since then, several editions of lithographs have been published.

164

"Rathmore," the Everard home, is situated in Kennedy Gardens. Built in 1861 for Andrew Aikman, a founder of the St. Andrews Civic Association, its uppermost window affords a view of some 60 miles to the Grampian Range. That view also enabled Annie Everard, wife of H.S.C., to search the links with a spyglass to ascertain his position on the golf course. With this information, she could instruct their cook when to begin preparing dinner.

"It may be safely said that there is now no one who plays his match from start to finish…more truly in the real golfing spirit and temper."

— Golf Illustrated *on H.S.C. Everard, 1901*

Harry Sterling Crawford Everard — often referred to by his initials "H.S.C." — is best remembered for his two books on golf: A History of the Royal and Ancient Golf Club *(1907) and* Golf: In Theory and Practice *(1896). Although he excelled at cricket while attending Oxford, golf became his preferred pastime. He was raised in England, but married into the famous Boothby family of golfers and moved to St. Andrews. An energetic member of the R & A, Everard played well enough to win the Silver Cross, Calcutta Cup and Glennie Medal.*

166

James Condie is known in the annals of golf history as a founder of the Royal Perth Golfing Society in 1824, a medal winner at the R & A, and patriarch of a prominent golfing family. In the 1850s, his challenge to play a match against any father and three sons went unanswered, perhaps because his son George was such an excellent player. The elder Condie was a solicitor, and there is still a legal firm in Perth that bears his name.

Major R.T. Boothby, was very active in St. Andrews golf during the second half of the 19th century. He learned the game from George Condie, brother of his bride-to-be, Annie. It was the Major who persuaded Old Tom Morris to return to his hometown of St. Andrews from his engagement at Prestwick in late 1864. Boothby, known for his gentleness and courtesy, was an accomplished golfer who held memberships at the R & A, Perth and Royal Blackheath. While noted for his excellence as a foursomes player, he also won several medals at stroke play. He died in 1897.

Angus Everard is a fifth-generation member of the Royal and Ancient Golf Club. Beginning with James Condie, his great-great-grandfather, subsequent generations consisted of Major Boothby, H.S.C. Everard and Angus' father, Hugo Everard. Although he is a physician in New Zealand, Angus still manages to visit his ancestral home of St. Andrews.

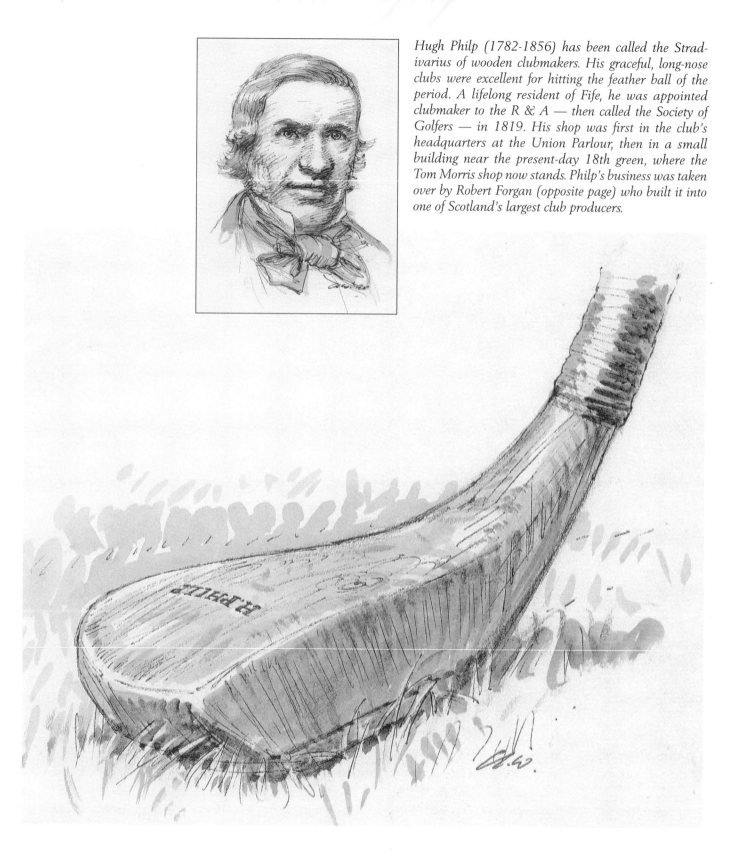

Hugh Philp (1782-1856) has been called the Stradivarius of wooden clubmakers. His graceful, long-nose clubs were excellent for hitting the feather ball of the period. A lifelong resident of Fife, he was appointed clubmaker to the R & A — then called the Society of Golfers — in 1819. His shop was first in the club's headquarters at the Union Parlour, then in a small building near the present-day 18th green, where the Tom Morris shop now stands. Philp's business was taken over by Robert Forgan (opposite page) who built it into one of Scotland's largest club producers.

168

Little is known about George Daniel Brown (above) except that he was one of the handful of contestants who played in the inaugural Open Championship in 1860, and that he ran a clubmaking shop for about five years in St. Andrews on the site occupied by Tom Morris' shop. Although recognized by golf historians as a bona fide clubmaker, only a few clubs marked "G.D. Brown" remain today.

Robert Forgan began working as a clubmaker for his uncle, Hugh Philp, in 1852. When Philp died four years later, Forgan took over the business, which eventually became R. Forgan & Son in 1881. The shop also produced gutty balls known for their expert hand-hammered finish circa 1860. Forgan was appointed clubmaker to the Prince of Wales in 1863. When the prince became King Edward VII in 1901, shortly after Forgan's death, the firm continued as royal clubmaker, earning the right to stamp all of its clubs with a mark of the crown. By the 1930s the firm had about 100 employees; it was eventually bought by Spalding, and relocated to Northern Ireland in 1962. The factory site, near the 18th green, is now home to the St. Andrews Woollen Mill (see page 41).

TOM STEWART: MASTER CLUBMAKER

Tom Stewart Jr. was one of the last clubmakers of the old school. After learning to hand forge iron heads from his father, a Carnoustie blacksmith, and Robert White, the noted clubmaker, Stewart decided to set up his own shop in St. Andrews in the early 1890s. A skilled blacksmith, he made everything from horseshoes to a special type of hole tin for greens.

Stewart's output was minimal when compared to Forgan's, the largest clubmaker in town. But his irons, with their unique pipe trademark, were top-of-the-line, and were exported throughout the world. Two of his most famous patrons were Francis Ouimet and Bobby Jones. He even took the liberty to stamp clubheads with "RTJ" or "FO/RTJ" to advertise his association with the champions.

His shop moved several times: from Market Street to Greyfriars Garden to Argyle Street. Stewart retired from clubmaking in 1931 and died a few weeks later. The firm continued under the leadership of his sons; later, it was taken over by Spalding.

A youthful Tom Stewart at his forge during the 1890s when iron clubs were fashioned with a hammer and anvil. He eventually mechanized his shop to keep up with the demand for his popular clubs.

The Stewart club factory was located on Argyle Street from the turn of the century until 1957, when production was combined with R. Forgan & Son at the latter's location on The Links. By that time, Spalding owned both historic firms.

Stewart enjoyed using, as well as making, golf clubs. He rarely missed his regular Saturday game and belonged to both St. Andrews Golf Club and the New Club, of which he was a founding member in 1902.

172

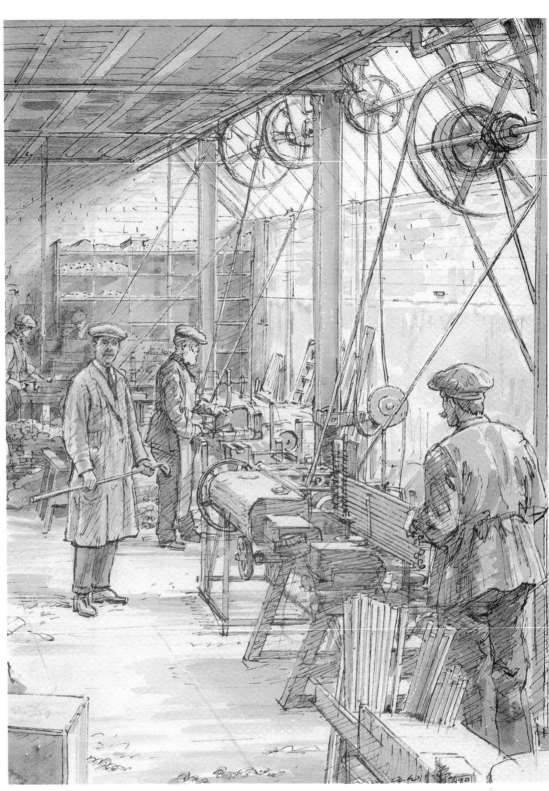

An early 20th-century scene from the Ellice Place workshop of D. Anderson & Sons, complete with belt-driven lathes and finishing machines.

David Anderson (left) was one of two sons of David "Old Da'" Anderson, the legendary 19th-century ballmaker, green-keeper and caddie. He oper-ated the clubmaking enterprise of D. Anderson & Sons, which flourished in St. Andrews from the mid 1890s until 1926. The Andersons were immersed in golf. All five of young David's sons worked in the family business. One of the sons, also named David, was an accom-plished player and finished second in the 1888 Open at St. Andrews. But it was Jamie, the eldest son of Old Da', who was the best golfer in the family; he was the Open champion thrice in succession in the 1870s.

174

The Tom Auchterlonie golf shop sits prominently at the corner of Golf Place and Pilmour Links. Tom (1879-1963) was the youngest brother of David and Willie, proprietors of the D. & W. Auchterlonie clubmaking firm. He initially worked for his brothers, but left in 1919 to open his own club business and relocated to Golf Place in 1935. Tom's son Eric became a partner in the business 20 years later and offered custom golf equipment until his retirement in 1986. No longer in family ownership, the shop continues to feature a full line of golf and other sporting goods. (This enterprise was unrelated to the clubmaking shop operated a few doors down Pilmour Links by Eric's first cousin Laurie. See page 187.)

◆

James Pett was the first known St. Andrews clubmaker. Diaries

show that he supplied clubs to the Duke of Montrose in 1628.

◆

A Plethora of Craftsmen

As the home of golf, St. Andrews has been home to many of the game's noteworthy clubmakers and ball-makers. Considering the relatively small size of the town and that, until 1896, it had only one golf course within its borders, it's incredible that the firms and individuals listed below all plied their trade in St. Andrews. This list includes just the prominent ones and not even those a few minutes away, such as George Nicoll in Leven or Alex Anderson in Anstruther.

After World War II, the number of makers in St. Andrews had dwindled to just a few. This was due to the worldwide growth of golf in the early 20th century, especially in the United States, where factories were needed to mass produce clubs and balls. Shops that remain today in St. Andrews are primarily retail establishments.

A partial listing of St. Andrews golf equipment makers include: Anderson & Blythe, David Anderson Sr., D. Anderson & Sons, Anderson & Gourlay, J. Anderson & Sons, Robert Anderson & Sons, Auchterlonie & Crosthwaite, D. & W. Auchterlonie, Tom Auchterlonie, James Beveridge, G.D. Brown, Robert Condie, David Dick, Robert Forgan & Son, Alex Herd, A. Jackson, Robert Kirk Sr., Robert Kirk Jr., Robert Martin, Watty McDonald, George Morris, Jack Morris, Tom Morris Sr., Tom Morris Jr., J.O.F. Morris, James Pett, Hugh Philp, Allan Robertson, Spence & Gourlay, Tom Stewart Jr., Andrew Strath, George Strath, Robert White, James Wilson, Robert Wilson, R.B. Wilson and Willie Wilson.

The British Golf Museum opened in 1990, after years of planning. Located across from the R & A clubhouse, the concrete and stone building offers patrons a variety of activities, ranging from displays of antique equipment to interactive video presentations.

Ted Holmes has caddied in St. Andrews for more than 30 years. Probably the most famous Scottish caddie of the 20th century is Tip Anderson, who has been associated with Arnold Palmer since 1960 (see page 102). In the last century, many of the best caddies also were the best players; Tom Morris, Allan Robertson and Tom Kidd were among those who supplemented their income as professional golfers by carrying clubs.

Caddies are required to register with the caddie manager before they may work the links. Badges have varied over the years; this early one is on exhibit at the Town Hall.

The flag at the caddie manager's office, near the first tee of the Old Course, is flown at half-mast during periods of mourning, including the death of a caddie.

In the late 19th century, legendary caddie David "Old Da'" Anderson operated a ginger beer stand on the ninth hole, where he would kibitz with golfers.

The R&A

THE ROYAL AND ANCIENT GOLF CLUB

178

The Royal and Ancient Golf Club of St. Andrews — universally known as the R & A — is golf's governing body except for in the U.S. and Mexico.

The clubhouse of the Royal and Ancient Golf Club majestically overlooks the first tee and 18th green of the Old Course. The imposing stone building opened in 1854, as a one-story structure, a century after the founding of the club. Previously, members met at the Union Parlour and before that, they gathered in various taverns.

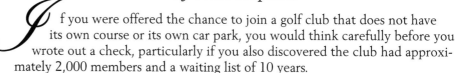

HISTORY AND TRADITIONS OF THE ROYAL AND ANCIENT GOLF CLUB

by John Hopkins

John Hopkins lives in London, where he is golf correspondent for The Times. *He also has written several golf books including* Golf: The Four Majors *and* Nick Faldo in Perspective.

*I*f you were offered the chance to join a golf club that does not have its own course or its own car park, you would think carefully before you wrote out a check, particularly if you also discovered the club had approximately 2,000 members and a waiting list of 10 years.

You wouldn't hesitate, though, if the club were the Royal and Ancient Golf Club of St. Andrews. Such is the popularity and prestige of the R & A that, given the chance, many golfers would join it tomorrow, sight unseen.

Is there another sport in the world that has become synonymous with one town? "It may be immoral but it is delightful to see a whole town given up to golf," noted Bernard Darwin, the golf writer, shortly after the turn of the century, "…to see the butcher and the baker and the candlestick maker shouldering his clubs as soon as his day's work is done and making a dash for the links."

As an attraction, the Old Course at St. Andrews is to golfers what the Vatican is to Catholics. Fifty thousand rounds, give or take a few, are played on it each year, and it could be open for 24 hours each day and still not satisfy demand.

Its influence spreads around the world. Though it was the Honourable Company of Edinburgh Golfers that drew up the first 13 rules of golf, it was to the R & A that it and other clubs turned in late Victorian times for a uniform set of rules. The R & A has continued ever since as the rule-making body for golf in every country except the United States and Mexico.

Golf was being played at St. Andrews before the mid-16th century. We know this because it was then that permission was confirmed by John Hamilton, the archbishop of St. Andrews, to breed and feed rabbits on the north part of the links, near the Eden Estuary, but only on the understanding that this did not interfere with the people's right to continue to play golf, football and shooting as they had for years.

The original course consisted of 22 holes, 11 out and 11 back. It started, so it is believed, from the St. Andrews cathedral wall and ran west to the estuary of the river Eden, a distance of nearly two miles.

A semblance of organization appeared in 1754 when 22 noblemen, landowners and gentlemen formed the Society of St. Andrews Golfers. Ten years earlier the Honourable Company of Edinburgh Golfers, the forefathers of the distinguished club now based at Muirfield, was formed. The St. Andrews club took a leaf out of the Honourable Company's book. In 1754, it started an annual competition for a Silver Club. The winner would become captain and attach a silver replica of the feathery ball he used to the Silver Club each year.

The captain had certain duties to fulfill. He had to settle any disputes, for example. One occurred in 1771 when a member pulled back his ball, presumably in frustration at missing a short putt. He was not disqualified. The captain decided the competition should be played again. The captain also had to oversee the maintenance of the links and make sure that coaches, chaises or other wheeled machines were forbidden to pass through the links.

Despite having to discharge these and other duties, some captains brought too light-hearted an approach to their responsibilities. In 1770, the Society instituted a system of fines. If the captain did not attend all the meetings throughout the year, he had to pay a fine of two pints of claret for every meeting he missed.

In 1834, the Society of St. Andrews Golfers changed its name. How and why it did so bears telling. In the previous year, King William IV bestowed royal patronage on the Perth Golfing Society, the first club to be so honored. When Murray Belshes, soon to be captain of the Society of St. Andrews Golfers, heard this, he wrote to the King's private secretary asking if the King, who was already Duke of St. Andrews, would agree to be patron of the club. It was agreed the following year, and the club thereafter became known as the Royal and Ancient Golf Club of St. Andrews.

Today it has a worldwide active membership approaching 2,000. Of this number, no more than 1,150 may live in Britain and Ireland and 750 may live overseas, of which no more than 275 can come from the United States. Three captains of the club have been American: Francis Ouimet, an amateur who, at age 20, stunned the world of golf by defeating Harry Vardon and Ted Ray, the two best British professionals, in a playoff for the 1913 U.S. Open at Brookline; Joe Dey, executive director of the United States Golf Association between 1935 and 1969, then commissioner of the PGA Tour until 1974, held office in 1976; and Bill Campbell, the former Walker Cup player and USGA president, who was captain in 1987.

In an article in *Sports Illustrated*, John Garrity wrote as follows about the club's membership. "The R & A has another history, of course — one full of shouts and cannon fire, as the portraits on the walls testify. Members have fired at Napoleon, fallen at Khartoum, marched with the Black Watch, died in trenches at the Somme, flown Spitfires for the RAF and walked on the moon. (Apollo astronaut Neil Armstrong and America's first man in space, Alan Shepard, are R & A members.) Generals have put their feet up in the Big Room; crowned heads of state have lunched on cold ham and tongue in the dining room; and the presidents of small nations have showered in the basement."

Alistair Cooke's pleasure at being asked to address the U.S. House of Representatives on the 200th anniversary of the First Continental Congress was diminished slightly by his having to cancel an engagement to speak at the annual dinner of the R & A the same night.

There is a certain mystique about the R & A. It comes in part from its setting, nearly 500 miles due north of London, in an area referred to as the Kingdom of Fife, as if it is a magical place in a children's fairy tale. St. Andrews has a cathedral, a medieval castle and Scotland's oldest university within its city limits. The place known as the "auld grey toun" is a mixture of town and gown. The presence of the students guarantees bookshops, cinemas, theaters, cheap restaurants and the general air of a place that does not close down at 8 p.m.

The mystique is not diminished by the aura surrounding the clubhouse, a two-story stone building that sits squarely behind the first tee and the 18th green. It can and does exert a sense of majesty that is almost tangible and induces feelings of nervousness in those who drive off from the first tee. A famous cartoon by H.M. Bateman, an English artist, depicts the ultimate golf disaster. It is entitled "The Man Who Missed the Ball on the First Tee at St. Andrews," and the original hangs near the men's locker room in the clubhouse.

"As an attraction, the Old Course at St. Andrews is to golfers what the Vatican is to Catholics."

181

♦

"If you were offered the chance to join a golf club that does not have its own course or its own car park, you would think carefully before you wrote out a check, particularly if you also discovered the club had approximately 2,000 members and a waiting list of 10 years."

♦

The prospect from the tee is a generous one. The combined width of the first and 18th fairways should make the opening drive one of the easiest in golf. However, nerves prey on the minds of those who drive off under the unforgiving gaze of the clubhouse and, as likely as not, a clutch of members standing in the Big Room of the clubhouse, drinks in hand.

One of the most distinctive records in amateur golf is held by the fellow who, with penalty strokes, took five strokes to get off the first tee of the Old Course. He hit his first out of bounds left and followed it by slicing his second ball out of bounds right. It happened at the Autumn Meeting of the R & A in 1992, and the members have not stopped talking about it yet.

The mystique of the R & A is further enhanced by the uniform worn by the captain: a red coat of office complete with medals, including a replica of the Queen Adelaide medal, presented by the widow of King William IV.

St. Andrews is teeming with ghosts. Old and Young Tom Morris are buried there. Bobby Jones, the legendary amateur, is as revered in the Scottish town as he ever was. There has been enough bloodletting through the centuries to satisfy Lady Macbeth. In 1543, a cleric was stabbed to death and his body hung from the walls of St. Andrews castle. For two centuries Protestants and Catholics were at one another's throats, and a gray stone obelisk behind the clubhouse of the R & A is a reminder of those bloody years.

It is a place of tradition and history, where rituals seem entirely appropriate. One ritual at St. Andrews is the closing of the Old Course on Sunday to give it a rest, and another is the playing of the course the other way round from time to time — by teeing off on the first and playing to the 17th green, from the second tee to the 16th green and so on.

It is fun. I did it once with Michael Bonallack, the secretary of the R & A. Again and again, we were presented with a new challenge in the midst of familiar surroundings. This led to confusion, such as when Bonallack stood on the 16th tee and aimed towards the 14th green and was actually playing the fourth hole. If you thought he was confused, then you should have seen me. I was about to chip to what I thought was the seventh green when a voice stopped me in my tracks. "Oi," shouted Bonallack, pointing. "Over here. That's the 11th green." Not everything changed, though. The eighth, ninth, 10th and 11th holes are still played in traditional order.

The practice of playing the course the other way round (of playing the left-hand course) dates back to the days of the feathery ball, the short spoon and the Georgian kings. It is the way the game always used to be played at the home of golf. The Opens of 1873, 1876, 1879 and 1881 were all held on the left-hand course as was the 1886 British Amateur. Then the authorities faced a crisis: the course was getting worn out from overuse. They ordained that play should be over the right-hand course, and this quickly became accepted as the medal course.

However, it wasn't long before this course began to suffer from the pounding of feet as well. In 1906, *Golf Illustrated*, a British weekly publication, noted "the practice of alternating the left-hand course with the ordinary right-hand course has been re-adopted, and the turf already shows signs that the policy of change produces less wear and tear."

It does not happen very often — every 20 years or so at the most — and when it does it causes confusion. In January 1989, the last occasion the left-hand course was used, the secretary of the St. Andrews Links Trust reported: "I've just had a telephone call from someone in Japan who wanted to book a starting time. I explained to him that he would have to play the course backwards. He didn't speak very good English, and I think he thought I was taking the mickey."

What history the R & A clubhouse has seen! The great gray stone building was erected in 1854, added to in 1900 and is probably too small for all its needs today. Inside, on the floor above the Big Room is the office of the secretary of the R & A. In there he sometimes pours visitors a drink in a glass with the club crest on it. On the balcony outside his window is a telescope with which he can see to the far end of the course and beyond, almost to Leuchars.

The clubhouse stands as an enduring testimony to the resoluteness of the R & A. London will fall down when the ravens leave the Tower of London, according to legend. There is no similar legend attached to the R & A's clubhouse and its present site, but one feels that the day the R & A moves from this magnificent building, then that will be the day the game changes.

For the moment, happily, it survives, a fine monument to a magnificent game, a building in harmony with its surroundings, at one with the game with which it is such an important part. "On quiet days when nothing of moment is afoot and a few members drowse in their deep chairs," wrote Pat Ward-Thomas, the British golf writer, "...one might look through the tall windows and dream awhile. So peaceful is the scene...that it is hard to believe that almost every great golfer in the game's history has stood on the tee below and looked down the long fall of fairway to the hills beyond; and that on an upper floor the processes of guidance and government are constantly underway."

Long may it last!

184

Deep within the massive clubhouse are the members' locker room and a billiard room, where this unusual six-legged chair sits in a corner.

The center of the R & A clubhouse contains a monstrous chamber, aptly called the "Big Room." Measuring 50 feet by 26 feet, with ceilings nearly as high as it is wide, the room is a combination lounge, reading room, art gallery and locker area. At the far end are bay windows which command a panoramic view of the Old Course. The walls are adorned with life-size portraits of early club captains and notable personalities, including Tom Morris, Allan Robertson, Freddie Tait, the Prince of Wales (Edward VIII), Her Majesty Queen Elizabeth, the Hon. A.J. Balfour and Field Marshal Earl Haig.

186

"St. Andrews is the only medieval town in Europe whose silhouette hasn't changed for 400 years. From the ninth tee of the Old Course, looking back toward the town, you see just what Mary, Queen of Scots, saw when she played golf there."

— Bill Campbell

Perhaps the finest views of the links are from the second-floor balcony of the R & A clubhouse. Looking south across the 18th green (above), one can see how really close the shops border the Old Course. Straight out from the balcony sits the first tee.

FAMOUS CAPTAINS

1863
THE PRINCE OF WALES

1876
PRINCE LEOPOLD

1884
GEORGE GLENNIE

1894
SIR A.J. BALFOUR, MP

1906
LESLIE BALFOUR-MELVILLE

1908
HORACE HUTCHINSON

1910
SAMUEL MURE FERGUSSON

1920
FIELD MARSHAL EARL HAIG

1922
THE PRINCE OF WALES

1930
THE DUKE OF YORK

1934
BERNARD DARWIN

1937
THE DUKE OF KENT

1946
ROGER WETHERED

1948
CYRIL TOLLEY

1951
FRANCIS OUIMET

1975
JOSEPH C. DEY JR.

1991
JOSEPH B. CARR

George Glennie is remembered for the medal bestowed in his honor by the Royal Blackheath Golf Club to the R & A. First awarded in 1882, the Glennie Medal is presented today to the R & A member who returns the lowest aggregate score for the Spring and Autumn meetings. Winners of the medal include some of the club's most prominent members: Horace Hutchinson, Leslie Balfour-Melville, H.S.C. Everard, Freddie Tait, John Low, Robert Maxwell, Leonard Crawley and Cyril Tolley. Glennie, the longtime honorary secretary and treasurer at Royal Blackheath, was elected captain of the R & A in 1884. He was a fine player; the record 88 he shot in the 1855 Autumn Medal stood for nearly three decades.

James Wolfe Murray, of Cringletie, was captain in 1848. He was known for being a prankster and was often seen riding his pony around town and on the links.

The Duke of York (later to become George VI) was one of the better golfers in the royal family. When the Duke drove himself in as captain in 1930, he impressed onlookers by hitting a formidable tee shot down the first fairway. (For more about the driving-in ritual, see page 193.)

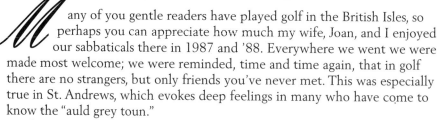

ESSAY

A HOLY PLACE FOR GOLFERS

by William C. Campbell

190

Bill Campbell, an insurance executive from Huntington, West Virginia, holds the distinction of being the only person elected captain of the R & A (1987) and president of the U.S. Golf Association (1983). On the golf course, he has enjoyed a lengthy competitive career, winning important titles for more than 30 years. In addition to capturing the 1964 U.S. Amateur and the 1979 and '80 U.S. Senior Amateurs, Campbell played on eight Walker Cup teams between 1951 and '75. He also qualified for 15 U.S. Opens and played in 18 Masters Tournaments.

Many of you gentle readers have played golf in the British Isles, so perhaps you can appreciate how much my wife, Joan, and I enjoyed our sabbaticals there in 1987 and '88. Everywhere we went we were made most welcome; we were reminded, time and time again, that in golf there are no strangers, but only friends you've never met. This was especially true in St. Andrews, which evokes deep feelings in many who have come to know the "auld grey toun."

The story is told that during World War II, with the Battle for Britain at its bleakest, an "old boy" — despairing of the outcome — traveled from London to St. Andrews. He went to the back parlor of Rusack's Hotel, where he peered through the big windows out to the West Sands and the North Sea beyond. In the foreground was what, in better days, had been the fairway for the first and last holes of the Old Course, then closed. Towards the beach he could see tank traps designed to impede an expected German invasion. Then his eye was caught by the outline of a solitary figure on hands and knees, just beyond the Swilcan Burn, weeding what had been the first green. The "old boy" took heart and returned to London, sharing with everyone his new confidence that Britain would prevail after all.

St. Andrews means different things to different people: the ancient ecclesiastical capital of Scotland, the home of the oldest Scottish university, a fine seaside resort, one of the most interesting and historic towns in Britain, and the "mecca of the world of golf." Also, more than any other place, St. Andrews combines the three bastions of Scottish history: Christianity, scholarship and golf (Scotland's second religion).

It is, indeed, a fascinating and beguiling place. While there, my wife and I lived in a house dating from 1480, attended a church that had been in town since 1112 and on the same site since 1415, and played golf on grounds where the game has been played for more than 500 years. St. Andrews is the only medieval town in Europe whose silhouette hasn't changed for 400 years. From the ninth tee of the Old Course, looking back toward the town, you see just what Mary, Queen of Scots, saw when she played golf there. And when you cross the Swilcan Burn on the 18th hole, you know the Stone Bridge was used by the Romans 800 years ago.

Any golfer on pilgrimage to St. Andrews gets, by observation and osmosis, a sense of the abiding admiration, even reverence, for the great players of the game who have played there — from Old Tom Morris and Young Tom to Bob Jones and Jack Nicklaus, among others — and for the kinds of people they were and are.

The outstanding champions have given golf a special heritage which deserves to be nurtured, honored and emulated wherever the game is played. We are talking about character, respect for the game, and courtesy to opponents, fellow competitors, officials and spectators. Golf is indeed unique; let's keep it that way.

When Bill Campbell became captain of the R & A in 1987, he joined Joe Dey and Francis Ouimet as the only Americans to hold this distinguished position. He and Dey (left) posed in their ceremonial captain's coats for this portrait by Arthur Weaver, which was commissioned by the USGA.

192

Upon driving himself in as captain of the R & A in 1951, Francis Ouimet awarded a gold coin to Arthur Speight, the caddie who retrieved the ball. As the first American captain, Ouimet broke tradition and presented a U.S. five-dollar gold piece (above left) rather than the customary British sovereign. The 1913 date signifies the date that Ouimet won his most important championship, the U.S. Open, by defeating Englishmen Harry Vardon and Ted Ray in a playoff. Ouimet, who also won the U.S. and French Amateur championships, was a stockbroker at the time of his captaincy.

The ceremonial driving-in ceremony is punctuated by the blast of a cannon at the moment the ball is struck.

THE DRIVING-IN CEREMONY

by John Hopkins

The most famous ritual of the Royal and Ancient Golf Club is the driving-in ceremony by the incoming captain, which takes place at 8 a.m. on the last morning of the Autumn Meeting. With one stroke, accompanied by the firing of a nearby cannon, the captain-elect drives himself into office.

The procedure, honed by years of tradition, is as follows. The retiring captain probably offers his successor a stiff drink in the clubhouse just before they walk to the first tee where the club's honorary professional tees up the ball. The members attending the Autumn Meeting have gathered around the tee. Meanwhile, down the fairway, caddies are jostling for position, each anxious to retrieve the ball and receive the traditional reward of a gold sovereign.

Many captains-elect have been unnerved. When one missed the ball completely, Willie Auchterlonie, the professional, being a quick thinker, stepped forward and said quietly, "A good practice swing, sir. Now just hit it." In 1922, the Prince of Wales (later Edward VIII) caught the ball with the nose of his driver, and it scattered spectators and crashed into a fence 50 yards away.

GOLF SCRIBE CHERISHED ASSOCIATION WITH THE R & A

by Jean Ward-Thomas

Pat Ward-Thomas (1913-1982) was one of Britain's most respected golf writers. He covered golf for the Manchester Guardian *for most of his career and also wrote for* Country Life. *He wrote several golf books, including* The Royal and Ancient, *a history of the R & A. His wife, Jean Ward-Thomas, penned the following recollections a month before her death in December 1992.*

194

I shall never forget the look of pleasure on my husband's face one morning at breakfast when he read me a letter. Pat's correspondent wished to know whether he would like to be put up for membership at the Royal and Ancient Golf Club.

It was a wonderful offer, of course. It had been a dream that Pat nurtured since childhood. Pat's parents were keen golfers, and it followed quite naturally that he should play. During a family golfing holiday in Scotland, his father took him to St. Andrews, and the role of the R & A was explained to him. The course and the clubhouse, both repositories of much history and tradition, made a strong impression on the boy. He told his father he would be a member one day. It was pointed out that membership was not acquired through normal channels, but bestowed by others. Rank and wealth were not considerations; achievement, a gentle upbringing, and a love and respect for the game were. A first lesson in humility was not lost on the boy and may have shaped his life to some extent.

Pat became a member in 1960. He had been *The Guardian*'s golf correspondent since 1950. (The quality of his writing undoubtedly played no small part in his selection for membership.) Henceforth, covering events at St. Andrews would be all the more pleasurable. The wearing of the plain but distinctive tie, the brass buttons on the blazer, the freedom of movement within the hallowed clubhouse, mixing with other members on equal footing, were regarded as great privileges.

The first of numerous championships he covered at St. Andrews was the 1950 Amateur Championship — won by Frank Stranahan. Over the years, his knowledge of and respect for the Old Course grew and inspired his writing. Traveling north to St. Andrews was always an occasion of special significance.

Pat wrote about the course in *The World Atlas of Golf*: "...every golfer there ever was has wanted to play at St. Andrews, and down the years it has attracted more pilgrims than any other course in the world. At first sight, the Old Course may not seem remarkable. One will have been charmed by the intimacy of its approaches from within the city and the beauty of the spacious rectangle of green, sweeping down from the Royal and Ancient clubhouse, gray four-square and slightly forbidding. On one side are the smaller clubs, Old Tom Morris' shop, hotels and houses; on the other a rolling sward of putting green and, beyond, the superb bay, leagues and leagues of golden sand curving away towards the distant estuary of the Tay. The Old Links has been condemned as an anachronism and cursed as being unfair, but no course has commanded greater affection and respect from those who have learned to appreciate its subtleties and charms…"

The World Amateur Championship in 1958 gave Pat the chance to meet his greatest hero, Bobby Jones, who was captain of the American team. Jones had set off in his electric buggy; the batteries ran out at the 13th and he was left stranded. Pat was among the spectators and with others did what he could to help until new batteries arrived. Pat cherished the memory of that meeting till he died. After his return to the United States, Jones wrote in a delightful letter, "…I want to tell you what a big help you were to me at St. Andrews and how very much I enjoyed our knocking around together. I am only sorry that I had to give you so much physical activity…"

A friendship developed and there were subsequent meetings in the States during Masters Tournaments — and I had the good fortune to be there. Over the years it was sad to see the progress of illness, but Jones was always charming and uncomplaining. We both felt proud to have known him.

All Opens are memorable, but some are more so. One such was in 1964, the year Tony Lema won. He came to St. Andrews, never before having played in Europe. He allowed himself 36 hours to get the feel of the course — many regarded it as folly if not irreverence. "Champagne" Tony lived up to his reputation, though, and I remember cases of champagne being brought to the press tent after his victory. Pat looked forward to several more years of writing about a gifted, intelligent player. Sadly, within two years Lema was dead, killed in a flying accident.

Pat felt it was fitting when Britain and Ireland won the Walker Cup on the Old Course in 1966. Going into the afternoon matches on the last day, Britain and Ireland needed 5$\frac{1}{2}$ points from eight singles for victory. Pat walked out on the course expecting to watch an academic American exercise, even though the scoreboards showed slightly in Britain's favor. One after another the British conquerors came into the timeless setting of Old Tom Morris' green — the 18th — with thousands gathered against the fences, on roofs and balconies, at windows and on the fairways. Cheers and tears of joy, relief and pride were mingled as they had not been for many years.

Another struggle that Pat vividly remembered on the Old Course was the playoff between Jack Nicklaus and Doug Sanders for the Open in 1970. The failure of Sanders to clinch victory in the last round by holing from a yard had no parallel in modern Open golf. Twenty-four hours later Nicklaus peeled off a sweater on the 18th tee, an unwittingly theatrical gesture, and unleashed an enormous drive which raced through the green into clinging grass. He squeezed his ball out of the rough to six feet; his putt, on the same line as Sanders' the previous evening, just held the break — for victory.

To be a member of a club of one's choosing is an honor and an achievement. To be a member of the R & A is the envy of many, but there is a price to pay: the member's first drive in the Autumn Medal competition. Pat approached it with fear because, without fail, friends and foes watch from the clubhouse, glass in hand, a bet at the ready, that the first drive will be a disaster.

The Old Course is a place for many kinds of memories: happy and sad, but all fulfilling.

"Over the years, his knowledge of and respect for the Old Course grew and inspired his writing. Traveling north to St. Andrews was always an occasion of special significance."

196

Alistair Cooke — internationally celebrated journalist, author, and radio and television personality — has been a member of the R & A since 1969. Born in Manchester, Cooke became a U.S. citizen in 1941 and now resides in New York. He received an honorary degree from the University of St. Andrews in 1975.

John Campbell of Saddell, shown with his daughters, was a wealthy and influential golfer in the 19th century, who had a passion for making wagers on the links. He is depicted as one of the players in the famous painting, "The Golfers" (see page 162). Although his domain was Saddell, located on an island off the coast of Glasgow, Campbell kept a residence in St. Andrews to be close to golf. This mid-19th century feather ball (right), bearing Campbell's personal imprint, is a rare link to the past. Documents show that the ball, now in a private collection, was once owned by St. Andrews caddy Bob Kirk and noted golfer Major Boothby.

Several U.S. presidents have ties to St. Andrews. Franklin Roosevelt played golf there on his honeymoon in 1905. Dwight D. Eisenhower and George Bush were both elected honorary members.

197

Graeme Summer was chairman of the Championship Committee from 1988 to 1991. He is currently chairman of the Scottish Sports Council.

William C. Battle, an overseas member from Virginia, served as president of the USGA from 1984 to 1987. He is a retired textile industry executive and was once U.S. ambassador to Australia. As a Navy officer during World War II, Battle helped to rescue Lt. John F. Kennedy after the loss of his craft, PT 109.

Bobby Ferber, a retired solicitor from Blackheath, near London, is a past chairman of the Rules of Golf Committee. He is past captain of Royal St. George's Golf Club and Royal Blackheath Golf Club, where he presently holds the position of field marshal.

◆

"The R & A is one club that no one ever drops out of — for any reason — except maybe death."

— Robert Trent Jones

◆

FOND MEMORIES

by Robert Trent Jones

I am privileged to have some very fond memories of St. Andrews, as I've been a member of the Royal and Ancient Golf Club since 1956. It is about the most coveted club membership a man could have in his lifetime, and to play the Old Course is a never-to-be forgotten occasion.

I am reminded of a story about a friend of mine who told his secretary that since he was retiring it was really not necessary to keep up membership in all of the many clubs to which he belonged. He asked her to weed out some of them. She was very prompt in carrying out his request and canceled most of the memberships, including the Royal and Ancient. She thought since it was overseas he might not have the opportunity to go there often.

You can imagine how horrified he was to hear that he was no longer a member. The R & A is one club that no one ever drops out of — for any reason — except maybe death. He can't get back in because of the long waiting list for membership. From that moment on, I made sure everyone on my staff knew that they should never, never do such a thing to me.

For some 200 years, the Royal and Ancient has administered the Rules of Golf. No one has ever attempted to deviate significantly from these traditional and accepted principles. You can say, therefore, that it is because of the Royal and Ancient that we all enjoy such a challenging and fascinating sport today.

I have certainly been inspired in designing and building my courses throughout the world by what I have seen at St. Andrews. Years ago, we never dreamed of using sand to aerate the greens as St. Andrews has always done. But when I was building a golf course in Puerto Rico — an area that was all sand — I thought of St. Andrews. As a result, we used the sand base to grow the turf, and the course turned out to be one of my most beautiful.

Now, USGA agronomists specify the use of sand for greens on all the new courses being built. They finally decided that this was the only way to make the greens so lush, firm and beautiful.

The most fascinating aspect of St. Andrews is how the Old Course has withstood the test of time. I may have been lauded for the courses I've built all over the world, but no one has come close to duplicating the Old Course. We just cannot capture the mystique that surrounds it.

Trent, as he is known to friends, is the dean of modern golf course architects. He has worked on about 500 courses in more than 30 countries. Jones was born in Ince, England, and immigrated to the United States as a child. He was once a scratch golfer.

A DESIGNING FAMILY

Robert Trent Jones has two sons. Both worked for their father before forming their own golf architecture firms. All three are overseas members of the Royal and Ancient Golf Club.

Robert Trent Jones Jr., known as "Bobby," lives in California, where he has access to his many jobs in the Pacific Basin. He recently authored Golf By Design, *which shows golfers how to improve their score by analyzing the features of a golf course.*

Rees Jones has designed or redesigned more than 100 courses, including the remodeling of several U.S. Open venues. He is based in Montclair, New Jersey and, like his father and brother, is a past president of the American Society of Golf Course Architects.

GOLF'S HOME IS MY HOME

by Michael Bonallack

My first view of St. Andrews and the Old Course was, like so many visitors before me, from the train which ran between Leuchars — where it met the overnight sleeper from London — and the town of St. Andrews. The occasion was the 1958 British Amateur Championship to be played on the Old Course. The memory of not only the championship itself, but in particular my first sight of the Old Course with the ancient town buildings silhouetted in the background by the rising sun, has stayed with me ever since.

Without a doubt, the name "M.F. Bonallack" is the most frequent entry in the record books of modern British amateur golf. After taking the British Boy's title in 1952, he won nearly every title of note, including the British and English Amateur championships five times each. He also represented his country on nine consecutive Walker Cup teams from 1957 to 1973. In 1983, following a decade in the golf course business, Bonallack assumed his current position as secretary to the R & A, where he oversees all operations of the club. Originally from Essex, he and his wife, Angela — also an accomplished golfer — consider St. Andrews their home.

I had no idea what to expect prior to this, and I was immediately struck by the fact that the course itself started almost in the heart of the town, bordered by buildings along one side and the sea on the other. The holes meandered out into open countryside before returning once again to the shadow of the imposing Royal and Ancient clubhouse.

From the minute I stepped from the train, I was aware of the unique character of the place. Practically everyone seemed to be dressed for golf, and in the short walk from the station to The Scores Hotel, it seemed every building I passed was connected with golf. Famous names were in the fasciae: Auchterlonie, Forgan, Tom Morris, and so on. It was as if I were stepping back in golf history.

To stand on the first tee of the Old Course, even in a practice round, was a daunting experience. In front was the widest fairway you could imagine. From behind, the critical eyes of the R & A members watched every swing, and their expressions reflected their assessment of each golfer's ability.

The gods, I am pleased to say, looked kindly on me and I progressed safely into the third round of the Amateur, thanks to a bye in the first. Just before the start of the third round, I took delivery of a brand new driver which had been made for me in 24 hours by the Tom Morris Golf Shop alongside the 18th green. The driver was unusual because it had a blue head and weighed a hefty 15 ounces. I thought the extra weight would help to slow down my swing. I hurried straight from the shop to the grass area near the first fairway and hit about 20 practice shots into the beach before heading for the first tee.

Being young and impressionable at the time, I must have thought that any club bearing the name Tom Morris and made in St. Andrews could do no wrong, as for the next four rounds I drove the ball as never before. As a result, I suddenly found myself in the semifinal against one Joe Carr from Ireland.

200

For nine holes the charmed spell continued; I was out in 33 and 2-up. Life was great. Then, turning for home and suddenly seeing the buildings of the town in the distance, I began to realize what an enormous effrontery I had. Here I was, standing on the 12th tee of the most famous golf course in the world in the semifinal of the Amateur Championship with a lead over a player whom I had held in awe ever since I began to play the game. Needless to say, the dream ended prematurely and, along with it, the match. Joe went on to win his second Amateur.

Nearly 40 years later it seems like yesterday. Little did I imagine then that in the years to come I would find myself with my office in that gray stone building looking out daily onto the scene that, for that one particular week, had been my inspiration and strengthened my interest in and love of the game of golf.

My second Amateur Championship over the Old Course in 1963 was not so successful. I lost in the fourth round. But the Walker Cup played there in 1971 was to provide me with one of the most memorable and happiest times I have experienced during my golfing life.

The Great Britain-Ireland team had only once won the Walker Cup — in 1938. Apart from a tied match in 1965, the results had been very one-sided and, for us, depressing. This was the fuel for my quest to be on a winning Walker Cup team before retiring from international competition. What better venue could there be than the Old Course, the scene of our only win, and what greater incentive and honor could I have been given than to be made playing captain?

As always, the American team was formidable, with names which have since become familiar to golfers worldwide: Tom Kite, Lanny Wadkins, Steve Melnyk, Vinny Giles, Bill Campbell, Bill Hyndman, and so on. Our team was largely unknown, although it did contain a Carr — Roddy, son of Joe.

One well known English golf writer, who currently commentates for an American TV network, even wrote that if the British team were to win he would gladly throw himself fully clothed into the Swilken Burn.

Well, win we did, but when the caddies went looking for the writer, it was learned that he had crawled out of the back of the press tent and beat a hasty retreat. What a night of celebration followed! St. Andrews never slept that night as practically every bar in town was filled to capacity.

Now St. Andrews is my home. Most of the buildings are the same as during my first visit, although some shops have different names. The railway line has long since gone, and in place of the coal yard, there is the luxurious Old Course Hotel with its magnificent views of the golf courses and St. Andrews Bay. The caddies are as knowledgeable as ever, the people as warm and as welcoming, but above all there remains the deep understanding and love for the game of golf. That, to my mind, is the essential essence of St. Andrews and why it will always be regarded as the "Home of Golf."

◆

"To stand on the first tee of the Old Course, even in a practice round, was a daunting experience."

◆

George Wilson is deputy secretary of the R & A. He has been associated with the club since 1973, and also acts as secretary to the Finance Committee and the Implements and Ball Committee.

202

For 14 years, the first person encountered by thousands of visitors to the R & A clubhouse was Tom Wallace, the hall porter. Until his retirement in 1993, Wallace ensured privacy at the club entrance and assisted members with their various needs. His place has been filled by Bob Marshall.

Members of the Grace family, including Stuart Grace (above), have provided years of service to R & A. Since many were named either Charles or Stuart, it's sometimes difficult to follow the lineage. Stuart's grandfather, also named Stuart, was secretary to the club from 1781 until his death in 1812, at which time his son Charles took over. He died in 1837. Our subject was secretary from 1842 until he retired in 1884, at which time the club decided to make the job a salaried one. Unable to find a suitable replacement, they asked Stuart to return. Using the funds for administrative assistance, he carried on until 1899. To further confuse the issue, three further generations — C.S. Grace, C.L.P. Grace and C.D.B. Grace — held the position of honorary treasurer in succession.

HONORARY GOLF PROFESSIONALS TO THE R & A

	YEARS OF SERVICE
TOM MORRIS SR. (SEE PAGE 78)	1865-1908
ANDREW KIRKALDY	1910-1934
WILLIE AUCHTERLONIE	1935-1963
LAURIE AUCHTERLONIE	1964-1987
JOHN PANTON	1988-

Andrew "Andra" Kirkaldy was a fine player and frequent contender for the Open Championship. At the end of the 19th century, he had seven top-10 finishes, including a playoff loss to Willie Park Jr. at Musselburgh in 1889. In two Championships held on the Old Course — in 1879 and 1891 — he also finished second. Kirkaldy succeeded Tom Morris as professional to the R & A in 1910.

The Auchterlonie name has been synonymous with golf in St. Andrews for more than a century. Brothers Laurence, Willie, David and Tom were the most famous of the six brothers and two sisters born to a local plumber. Laurence spent much of his career as a professional in the United States, and won the U.S. Open in 1902. Willie, winner of the 1893 British Open, was best known as a clubmaker. Originally an apprentice to Robert Forgan, he set up shop in St. Andrews after his Open win. Initially, the firm operated as Auchterlonie & Crosthwaite, but became D. & W. Auchterlonie in 1897 when Crosthwaite left and Willie was joined by his brother David. Tom had his own business (see page 174). Willie taught the clubmaking craft to his son, Laurie (1904-1987), who continued to handcraft clubs and sell golf goods at the shop on Pilmour Links. For more than half a century, first Willie, then Laurie, served as honorary professional to the R & A. In 1983, the club made Laurie an honorary member.

CREDITS

Our thanks to those who provided the featured essays. Special thanks to Herbert Warren Wind, Sidney Matthew and John Hopkins for their respective articles on the Old Course, Bobby Jones' visits to St. Andrews, and the Royal and Ancient Golf Club. The following also provided assistance: Michael Bonallack, Ken Bowden, Jeremy Campion, Century Hutchinson (for Wethered essay), Barbara Ferguson, Bobby Ferber, John W. Fischer III, Alastair J. Johnston, Ralph W. Miller Golf Library, the Royal and Ancient Golf Club, St. Andrews & N.E. Fife Tourist Board, St. Andrews Links Trust, Margaret Tait and the University of St. Andrews Library.

Layout: Joel Williams, Chelsea Design

Design: Patti Weller Bresler

Editing: Mary Friedberg
Chas. A. "Bud" Dufner

Research: Gordon Christie
Grace Donald
Robert Smart

SELECTED BIBLIOGRAPHY

Burnett, Bobby. *The St. Andrews Opens*
Cant, R.G. *The University of St. Andrews*
Darwin, Bernard. *The Golf Courses of the British Isles*
Everard, H.S.C. *A History of the Royal and Ancient Golf Club*
Fife Golfing Association. *A History of Golf Clubs in Fife*
Henderson, Ian T. and Stirk, David I. *Golf in the Making*
Hutchinson, Horace G. *Fifty Years of Golf*
Knott, C.G. *Life and Scientific Work of P.G. Tait*
Lamont-Brown, Raymond. *The Life and Times of St. Andrews*
Low, John L. *F.G. Tait: A Record*
Lyle, David W. *Shadows of St. Andrews Past*
Olman, John M. and Olman, Morton W. *The Encyclopedia of Golf Collectibles*
Olman, John M. and Olman, Morton W. *Golf Antiques and Other Treasures of the Game*
Robertson, James K. *St. Andrews: Home of Golf*
Robertson, James K. *About St. Andrews*
Ryde, Peter. *Royal and Ancient Championship Records*
St. Andrews Preservation Trust. *St. Andrews*
Salmond, J.B. *The Story of the R & A*
Steel, Donald and Ryde, Peter. *The Encyclopedia of Golf*
Taylor, Dawson. *St. Andrews: Cradle of Golf*
Ward-Thomas, Pat. *The Royal and Ancient*

Various editions of the following periodicals:
Dundee Courier
Golf (London)
Golf Illustrated (UK)
The Golfer's Handbook
Golfweek
The New York Times
PGA Tour Media Guide
St. Andrews Citizen
A Year at St. Andrews

NOTE: **Bold** entries denote illustrations.